Hooked on Shakespeare

HERBERT PRESS
Bloomsbury Publishing Plc
50 Bedford Square, London, WC1B 3DP, UK
29 Earlsfort Terrace, Dublin 2, Ireland

BLOOMSBURY, HERBERT PRESS and the Herbert Press logo
are trademarks of Bloomsbury Publishing Plc

First published in Great Britain in 2023

A catalogue record for this book is available from the British Library

ISBN: 978-1-7899-4128-9; eBook: 978-1-7899-4127-2

2 4 6 8 10 9 7 5 3 1

Produced and designed for Bloomsbury by Plum5 Limited
Edited by Rachel Vowles and Helen Welch
Photography by Andy Smart
Illustrations by Amelia Best
Step-by-step hand shots photographed by Nikol Dehaan and Najiyah Abdin
Work in progress photographs by Gurinder Kaur Hatchard

Printed and bound in China by C&C Offset Printing Co., Ltd.

To find out more about our authors and books visit www.bloomsbury.com
and sign up for our newsletters

Hooked on Shakespeare

Crochet Projects
Inspired by
The Bard

Gurinder Kaur Hatchard

H E R B E R T P R E S S
LONDON • OXFORD • NEW YORK • NEW DELHI • SYDNEY

Contents

To the three people I'm lucky to share my home and my world with, you all bring me so much joy, Kev, Maya and Rishi.

'I love you with so much of my heart that none is left to protest.'

Beatrice, *Much Ado About Nothing* (Act IV, Scene 1)

Introduction

The works of Shakespeare have inspired millions of people across the globe for hundreds of years. There have been countless interpretations of Shakespeare's plays throughout the centuries on the stage, screen, in books, paintings, and video games, and now crochet is getting in on the act.

It's an appealing subject, given that there are 37 plays and hundreds of characters to choose from. I love that there is a wealth of different settings including the ancient world, magical kingdoms, the dark ages and the Tudor era. Some of his characters are adored, others universally hated and many are complex. It was difficult to narrow it down to 30 characters from 14 of the plays, and of course I had to include William himself (or Woolliam as I've decided to rename him!).

Even if you've never read or watched one of his plays, it's likely you've quoted him without realising. Phrases like 'wild goose chase', 'cruel to be kind', 'eaten out of house and home' and 'be-all and end-all' are all from Shakespeare, as well as many more phrases we use in our everyday lives.

The patterns in this book are easy to follow, with step-by-step instructions, as well as pictures and charts to help you create your own Shakespearean characters using the amigurumi technique. If you've never crocheted before you'll find pictures to get you started and you'll also find videos on yayforcrochet.com. While you practise, remember that Lady Macbeth was wrong when she said 'What is done cannot be undone' (Act V, Scene 1), so keep going and just unpick when you need to.

The designs are inspired by the time the plays were set, they are not exact replicas, and dramatic licence has definitely been used. My aim was that they would be a joyful tribute to the Bard and easy to recreate in crochet rather than historically accurate.

Happy crocheting (or should that be cro-shakespearing?)!

Gurinder
xx

Getting Started

Yarns

The majority of the yarn used in this book is 4ply 100% cotton, although these patterns will convert well to other yarn types, like DK or Light Worsted yarn. If you use a different type of yarn your finished size will be different, and you'll also need to use a different hook size. I would recommend using the same weight of yarn for the same pattern.

Although I've suggested colours for clothes and skin tones, your creations will be unique to your work so play around with the colours and a brand you like and make them your own.

I have included the yarn colour you'll need and then followed with the exact yarn I've used. The brand I have used mostly in this book is Yarn and Colors Must Have, a Dutch company who ship internationally and, at the time of writing, have over 100 colours in their range: yarnandcolors.com.

Other recommended suppliers include Ricorumi, Drops, Paintbox or Patons – although this list is by no means exhaustive.

Hooks

Crochet hooks can be found in a few different materials including bamboo, plastic and aluminium. Good standard metal crochet hooks tend to be the easiest to get started with.

You'll generally find the size of the hook printed onto it in the middle.

If you're prone to repetitive strain injuries, a hook with an ergonomic handle may be best for you.

Most of the patterns in this book are created with either a 2.5 mm hook (C/2), which suits 4ply cotton well, but if you're using a different weight of yarn you will want to use an appropriately sized hook. My advice would be to use a slightly smaller hook than recommended, eg 3 mm (D/3) for DK or Light Worsted yarn so that your figures don't have many holes and are sturdy enough for being stuffed.

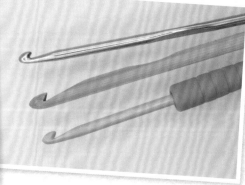

Tapestry Needle

These are blunt with a large eye for threading yarn through. You'll need these a lot throughout your work, sewing your pieces together, adding embellishments, basic embroidery and for weaving in those dreaded loose ends!

Scissors

Keep a pair handy with you for snipping your yarn – using your teeth as a substitute is not recommended!

Stitch Markers

When using the amigurumi technique, you'll need to mark the first stitch of every round. There are lots of adorable ones you can buy, but you could also use a piece of yarn in a contrasting colour.

Stuffing

All the figures will need stuffing. You can can easily buy polyester stuffing and there are some brands that make this from recycled materials, which is what I have used in this book. A zero-waste option would be to consider just saving all your little scraps of yarn that you've snipped off from other projects, or using old snipped-up clothes. If you're going to be using the figures as toys rather than for ornamental uses please check the guidelines to ensure that you're using stuffing that is safe for children.

'The web of our life is of a mingled yarn, good and ill together.'

All's Well That Ends Well (Act IV, Scene 3)

Wire

If you want to allow your figures to have some motion, and make them a bit sturdier, you may want to add wire.

2 mm PVC garden wire is recommended, along with small wire cutters and pliers.

Cut a length of around 25 cm, and fold over the ends with the pliers. Fold the wire in the middle. When you've joined the legs and have started on the main body, insert the ends into each of the legs and bend to fit the feet.

Twist the rest of the wire and continue to create the rest of the body and head around the wire.

For the arms, cut a 15 cm piece of wire, and take off the coating. Insert into one side and through the body to the other side. Fold one end over.

Add one of the arms to the folded end and sew the arm to the body. Repeat on the other side, you may need to slightly cut the wire to size.

Please note: this method is not recommended if your figures will be in reach of small children.

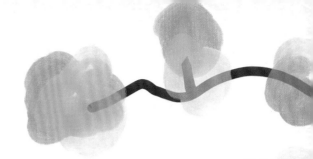

Safety Eyes

I have used 6 mm safety eyes throughout the book, but you may want to choose a different size to give your figures a different style or use different coloured yarn or thread to create the look instead.

For most of the characters I've used a small amount of black and white yarn to make the eyes look a bit more realistic.

To do this, while making the head, put both of the safety eyes through the head, without adding the back.

Use the white yarn and sew a small line around the lower outside half of both of the eyes.

Then use the black yarn and sew a small line along the higher outside half of both of the eyes.

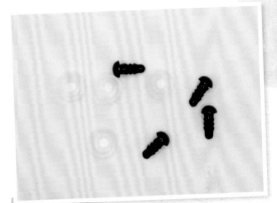

General Tips

Here are a few pointers to help you with creating the characters. For instructions on how to crochet for beginners, see page 116.

Legs

Most of the characters start from the feet and work upwards. To begin make 6ch, miss the first ch then work 1dc in each ch to the last ch, work 4dc in the last ch then turn and work back along the underside of the ch and work 3dc in the same ch that you worked your first dc, this is the end of the round so slip stitch to join.

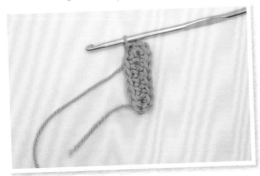

At the end of this round, slip stitch to join.

Begin round two in the next stitch, placing your marker so you know where you started *(see chart)*.

For the rest of the rounds, don't join, just work in spirals in the usual amigurumi style.

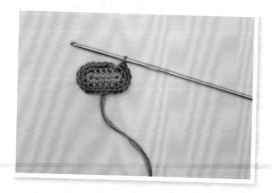

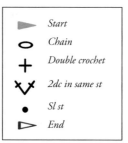

▶	Start
○	Chain
+	Double crochet
✕	2dc in same st
•	Sl st
▷	End

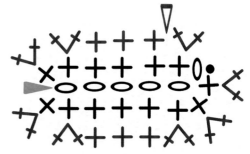

When you've finished a leg, slip stitch to neaten, and fasten off.

To join the legs, refasten your yarn to the left leg, so it lines up to the inside leg.

Crochet four chains and attach to the other side. 1dc into the next st, and place marker – this is where your round will start.

Arms

For neater arms, add a sl st as the final stitch and leave enough yarn to sew on.

Changing Colour

A neat way to change colour is to complete the final part of a stitch (pull the yarn through the loops) in the new colour.

This example shows a double crochet. This method will be particularly useful if making Macbeth's tartan.

Head

When on the last round of the head, you may find your decreasing stitches are difficult to continue with.

Instead you could just sew up the hole with a tapestry needle.

NOTES FOR ALL PATTERNS

Patterns are written using UK terms, but you'll find a conversion chart for US terms on page 127.

Unless otherwise stated:

- 1ch at the start of a row or round doesn't count as a st.

- 2ch at the start of a row or round counts as a htr.

- 3ch at the start of a row or round counts as a tr.

- Stuff the patterns as you go.

- Leave enough yarn for sewing the limbs, hair and other accessories.

Romeo and Juliet

'My only love sprung from my only hate,
Too early seen unknown, and known too late!'

Juliet (Act I, Scene 5)

Two youngsters from opposing families, both alike in dignity, fall in love and marry in secret. If that wasn't complicated enough, a fight breaks out between the two families and the groom ends up killing the bride's cousin. Juliet is meant to be marrying someone else, so fakes her own death to avoid it. Romeo hears the news that she has died, decides to poison himself next to her 'dead' body. Juliet wakes to find that Romeo is dead and also kills herself.

The play about the star-crossed lovers was inspired by the 1562 Arthur Brooke poem *The Tragicall Historye of Romeus and Juliet*. Brooke's story takes place over a few months rather than Shakespeare's few days, and Juliet is slightly older at 16, as opposed to just 13 in Shakespeare's version. The Bard's original title was *The Most Excellent and Lamentable Tragedy of Romeo and Juliet* – which certainly might be a bit more challenging to fit on theatrical posters.

YARN

100% cotton 4ply; royal blue, flesh, white, maroon, yellow, grey

SUGGESTED YARN:
'Must-have' from Yarn and Colors: Amethyst, Peach, White, Red Wine, Golden Glow, Shark Grey

OTHER MATERIALS

2.5 mm (C/2) crochet hook
Yarn needle
6 mm (1/3 in) safety eyes x 2
Stitch marker
Fibrefill stuffing

PATTERN NOTES

- For htrcl stitch instructions, see page 124.
- For hair instructions, see page 125.

Romeo

RIGHT LEG

With maroon yarn
Rnd 1: 6ch, 1dc in 2nd ch from hook, 3dc, 4dc in next st, work remaining sts along the other side of the chs, 3dc, 3dc in next st, join. (14)
Work in spirals in continuous rounds without joining (unless otherwise stated), moving stitch marker up each round.
Rnd 2: 3dc, [2dc in next st] 4 times, 3dc, [2dc in next st] 4 times. (22)
Rnd 3 *in blo*: 3dc, [dc2tog] 4 times, 3dc, [dc2tog] 4 times. (14)
Rnd 4: 2dc, [dc2tog] 4 times, 1dc in each st to end. (10)
Rnd 5: 2dc, [dc2tog] twice, 1dc in each st to end. (8)
With grey yarn
Rnd 6 *in blo*: 1dc in each st to end. (8)
Rnds 7-13: 1dc in each st to end. (8)

LEFT LEG, BODY AND HEAD

With maroon yarn
Rnd 1: 6ch, 1dc in 2nd ch from hook, 3dc, 4dc in next st, work remaining sts along the other side of the chs, 3dc, 3dc in next st, join. (14)
Work in spirals in continuous rounds without joining (unless otherwise stated), moving stitch marker up each round.

Rnd 2: 3dc, [2dc in next st] 4 times, 3dc, [2dc in next st] 4 times. (22)
Rnd 3 *in blo*: 3dc, [dc2tog] 4 times, 3dc, [dc2tog] 4 times. (14)
Rnd 4: 2dc, [dc2tog] 4 times, 1dc in each st to end. (10)
Rnd 5: 2dc, [dc2tog] twice, 1dc in each st to end. (8)
With grey yarn
Rnd 6 *in blo*: 1dc in each st to end. (8)
Rnds 7-13: 1dc in each st to end. (8)
Rnd 14: 4ch, join with a sl st to right leg, 1dc around right leg, then continue 1dc in each st across chs, around left leg, and across the other side of the chs. (24)
Rnds 15-16: 1dc in each st to end. (24)
With maroon yarn
Rnds 17-19: 1dc in each st to end. (24)
Rnd 20 *in blo*: 1dc in each st to end. (24)
Rnds 21-27: 1dc in each st to end. (24)
Rnd 28: [4dc, dc2tog] 4 times. (20)
Rnd 29: 1dc in each st to end. (20)
Rnd 30: [3dc, dc2tog] 4 times. (16)
Rnd 31: 1dc in each st to end. (16)
Rnd 32: [2dc, dc2tog] 4 times. (12)
With flesh yarn
Rnd 33: [1dc, dc2tog] 4 times. (8)
Rnd 34: 1dc in each st to end. (8)
Rnd 35: [2dc in next st, 1dc] 4 times. (12)
Rnd 36: 2dc in next st to end. (24)
Rnds 37-40: 1dc in each st to end. (24)

Rnd 41: 1dc in each st until you get to the middle of the face, 4htrcl in next st, 1dc in each st to end. (24)

Rnds 42-44: 1dc in each st to end. (24)
Attach eyes and use a little of the maroon yarn to create a mouth.
Begin to stuff

Rnd 45: [dc2tog, 2dc] 6 times. (18)
Rnd 46: [dc2tog, 1dc] 6 times. (12)
Rnd 47: dc2tog until hole closes.

TROUSERS
With royal blue yarn
Start in the front loops of rnd 18, begin at the middle of the back and work down Romeo.

Rnd 1: 1ch, 1dc in each st to end, join with sl st. (24)
Rnd 2: 2ch, 1htr in each st to end, join with sl st. (24)
Rnd 3: 2ch, 4htr, 2htr in next st, [5htr, 2htr in next st] 3 times, join with sl st. (28)
Rnds 4-5: 2ch, 1htr in each st to end. (28)
Rnd 6: 2ch, 12htr, fasten off, miss 1 st and then refasten the blue yarn, 2ch, 12htr, fasten off. (26)
Sew the middle part to form trousers.

JACKET
With royal blue yarn
Ch26

Row 1: 1htr in 3rd ch from hook, 1htr in each st to end, turn. (25)
Rows 2-3: 2ch, 1htr in each st to end, turn. (25)
Row 4: 2ch, 3htr, 2htr in next st, [4htr, 2htr in next st] 4 times, turn. (30)
Rows 5-8: 2ch, 1htr in each st to end, turn. (30)
Wrap jacket around body. For the jacket fastenings, create a large knot and use the needle to sew across to the other side of the jacket, pull through and create another large not on the other side. Repeat once.

ARMS
(Make 2)
With flesh yarn
Rnd 1: 8dc in magic ring. (8)

Rnds 2-4: 1dc in each st to end. (8)
With royal blue yarn
Rnds 5-14: 1dc in each st to end. (8)

CUFFS
(Make 2)
With white yarn
4ch
Row 1: 1dc in 2nd ch from hook, 1dc in each of next 2ch, turn. (3)
Rows 2-12 *in blo*: 1ch, 1dc in each st to end, turn. (3)
Attach cuffs to arms, sew arms onto side of body.

SHOULDERS
(Make 2)
With royal blue yarn
Row 1: 4ch, 1tr in first ch, work all subsequent stitches into the first ch, [*with maroon yarn*, 1tr, *with royal blue yarn* 1tr] 4 times, 1tr, don't turn or join. (11)
Leave a 10 cm strand of royal blue yarn for sewing. Rejoin maroon yarn on the same side right side facing.
Row 2: 1ch, 1dc in each st to end. (11)
Sew onto the top of arms.

RUFF
(Make 2)
With white yarn
Ch4
Row 1: 1dc in 2nd ch from hook, 1dc in each st to end, turn. (3)
Rows 2-27 *in blo*: 1ch, 1dc in each st to end, turn. (3)
Attach around neck.

HAIR
With brown yarn
Rnd 1: 6dc in magic ring. (6)
Rnd 2: 2dc in each st. (12)
Rnd 3: [2dc in next st, 1dc] 6 times. (18)
Rnd 4: [2dc in next st, 2dc] 6 times. (24)
Rnds 5- 8: 1dc in each st to end. (24)
Rnd 9: sl st in first st, [3ch, 1dc in first ch from hook, miss next st in rnd 8, sl st in next st] 8 times, sl st to neaten. (24)
Sew hair onto head.

'My lips, two blushing pilgrims, ready stand
To smooth that rough touch with a tender kiss.'

Romeo (Act I, Scene 5)

YARN

100% cotton 4ply; light blue, dark blue, flesh, black

SUGGESTED YARN:

'Must-have' from Yarn and Colors: Nordic Blue, Sapphire, Cigar, Black

OTHER MATERIALS

2.5 mm (C/2) crochet hook
Yarn needle
6 mm (1/3 in) safety eyes x 2
Stitch marker
Fibrefill stuffing

PATTERN NOTES

- For htrcl stitch instructions, see page 124.
- For surface crochet instructions, see page 123.

Juliet

RIGHT LEG

With light blue yarn
Rnd 1: 6ch, 1dc in 2nd ch from hook, 3dc, 4dc in next st, work remaining sts along the other side of the chs, 3dc, 3dc in next st, join. (14)
Work in spirals in continuous rounds without joining (unless otherwise stated), moving stitch marker up each round.
Rnd 2: 3dc, [2dc in next st] 4 times, 3dc, [2dc in next st] 4 times. (22)
Rnd 3 *in blo*: 3dc, [dc2tog] 4 times, 3dc, [dc2tog] 4 times. (14)
Rnd 4: 2dc, [dc2tog] 4 times, 1dc in each st to end. (10)
With flesh yarn
Rnd 5: 2dc, [dc2tog] twice, 1dc in each st to end. (8)
Rnds 6-13: 1dc in each st to end. (8)

LEFT LEG, BODY AND HEAD

With light blue yarn
Rnd 1: 6ch, 1dc in 2nd ch from hook, 3dc, 4dc in next st, work remaining sts along the other side of the chs, 3dc, 3dc in next st, join. (14)
Work in spirals in continuous rounds without joining (unless otherwise stated), moving stitch marker up each round.
Rnd 2: 3dc, [2dc in next st] 4 times, 3dc, [2dc in next st] 4 times. (22)

Rnd 3 *in blo*: 3dc, [dc2tog] 4 times, 3dc, [dc2tog] 4 times. (14)
Rnd 4: 2dc, [dc2tog] 4 times, 1dc in each st to end. (10)
With flesh yarn
Rnd 5: 2dc, [dc2tog] twice, 1dc in each st to end. (8)
Rnds 6-13: 1dc in each st to end. (8)
With light blue yarn
Rnd 14: 4ch, join with a sl st to right leg, 1dc in each st around right leg, then continue 1dc in each st across chs, around left leg and across the other side of the chs. (24)
Rnds 15-19: 1dc in each st to end. (24)
Rnds 20-21 *in blo*: 1dc in each st to end. (24)
Rnds 22-27: 1dc in each st to end. (24)
Rnd 28: [4dc, dc2tog] 4 times. (20)
Rnd 29: 1dc in each st to end. (20)
Rnd 30: [3dc, dc2tog] 4 times. (16)
Rnd 31: 1dc in each st to end. (16)
With dark blue yarn
Rnd 32: [2dc, dc2tog] 4 times. (12)
With flesh yarn
Rnd 33: [1dc, dc2tog] 4 times. (8)
Rnd 34: 1dc in each st to end. (8)
Rnd 35: [2dc in next st, 1dc] 4 times. (12)
Rnd 36: 2dc in each st to end. (24)
Rnds 37-40: 1dc in each st to end. (24)
Rnd 41: 1dc in each st, until you get to the middle of the face, 4htrcl in next st, 1dc in each st to end. (24)
Rnds 42-44: 1dc in each st to end. (24)
Add eyes, sew on a mouth.
With flesh yarn
Rnd 45: [dc2tog, 2dc] 6 times. (18)
Rnd 46: [dc2tog, 1dc] 6 times. (12)
Rnd 47: dc2tog until hole closes.

UNDERSKIRT

With dark blue yarn
Turn Juliet upside down and work into front loops of round 20. Join at any point.
Rnd 1: 2ch, 1htr in each st to end. (24)
Rnds 2-9: 2ch, 1htr in each st to end. (24)

> *'O Romeo, Romeo,*
> *wherefore art thou Romeo?*
> *Deny thy father and*
> *refuse thy name...*
>
> *Thou art thyself*
> *though not a Montague.*
> *What's Montague?'*
>
> Juliet (Act II, Scene 2)

OUTERSKIRT

With light blue yarn
Keeping Juliet turned upside down, work into front loops of round 21, start from 2sts to the left of the middle.

Row 1: 2ch, [2htr in next st, 1htr] 10 times, 2htr in the next st, leave the remaining 2sts in the middle unworked, turn. (32)

Row 2: 2ch, 3htr, [2htr in next st, 4htr] 5 times, 2htr in next st, 2htr, turn. (38)

Rows 3-9: 2ch, 1htr in each st to end, turn. (38)

ARMS

(Make 2)
With flesh yarn

Rnd 1: 8dc in magic ring. (8)
Rnds 2-4: 1dc in each st to end. (8)
With dark blue yarn
Rnds 5-14: 1dc in each st to end. (8)
Sew to side of body.

SLEEVES

(Make 2)
With light blue yarn
Ch3

Row 1: 5htr in first ch st, turn. (6)
Row 2: 2ch, [2htr in next st] 4 times, 1htr, turn. (10)
Row 3: 2ch, [2htr in next st, 1htr] 4 times, 1htr, turn. (14)
Row 4: 2ch, 1htr in each st to end. (14)
Surface crochet with dark blue across row 4. Wrap around top of arms and sew to body.

HAIR CAP

With black yarn

Rnd 1: 6dc in magic ring. (6)
Rnd 2: 2dc in each st. (12)
Rnd 3: [2dc in next st, 1dc] 6 times. (18)
Rnd 4: [2dc in next st, 2dc] 6 times. (24)
Rnds 5-8: 1dc in each st to end. (24)
Rnd 9: 1dc in each st to end, sl st to neaten. (24)

HAIR

(Make 16 or more if required)
With black yarn
Ch22
Fasten off.
Attach to hair cap at various points.
Sew onto head.

HEADDRESS

With light blue yarn
Ch3

Row 1: 9htr in first ch, turn. (10)
Row 2: 2ch, [2htr in next st] 8 times, 1htr, turn. (18)
Row 3: 2ch, [2htr in next st, 1htr] 8 times, 1htr, turn. (26)
Row 4: 2ch, 1htr in each st to end. (26)
Optional: Leave a long tail to keep hair wrapped up.
Surface crochet with dark blue yarn across row 3. Place on head.

Macbeth

'By the pricking of my thumbs,
Something wicked this way comes.'

Witches (Act IV, Scene 1)

Macbeth and his friend Banquo meet three witches while travelling home. They prophesy that Macbeth will become Thane of Cawdor and then King of Scotland, and Banquo's descendants will one day rule. When Macbeth returns home, the King promotes him to Thane of Cawdor, making him believe that the first prophecy has come true. He tells his wife and the pair plot to take the throne and kill anyone who gets in their way.

The foul tragedy is full of murder, betrayal, ambition, ghostly apparitions, paranoia and prophecy. Loosely based on Scottish history in the 11th century, it is likely to have been written to entertain Shakespeare's patron King James, who ruled Scotland and then inherited the English throne from Elizabeth I. King James was a strong believer in witchcraft, even writing a book on the subject called *Daemononlogie*, and he thought he was a descendent of Banquo.

YARN

100% cotton 4ply; brown, light grey, black, flesh, orange, blue, red, green, yellow

SUGGESTED YARN:

'Must-have' from Yarn and Colors: Brownie, Silver, Black, Peach, Bronze, Sapphire, Pepper, Peony, Mustard

OTHER MATERIALS

2.5 mm (C/2) crochet hook
Yarn needle
6 mm (1/3 in) safety eyes x 2
Stitch marker
Fibrefill stuffing

PATTERN NOTES

- For htrcl stitch instructions, see page 124.
- Use the instructions on page 23 for changing colours when making the tartan.
- Use the chart as a guide for the colour changes.

Macbeth

RIGHT LEG

With brown yarn

Rnd 1: 6ch, 1dc in 2nd ch from hook, 3dc, 4dc in next st, work remaining sts along the other side of the chs, 3dc, 3dc in next st, join. (14)

Work in spirals in continuous rounds without joining (unless otherwise stated), moving stitch marker up each round.

Rnd 2: 3dc, [2dc in next st] 4 times, 3dc, [2dc in next st] 4 times. (22)

Rnd 3 *in blo*: 3dc, [dc2tog] 4 times, 3dc, [dc2tog] 4 times. (14)

Rnd 4: 2dc, [dc2tog] 4 times, 1dc in each st to end. (10)

Rnd 5: 2dc, [dc2tog] twice, 1dc in each st to end. (8)

Rnds 6-8: 1dc in each st to end. (8)

With grey yarn

Rnd 9 *in blo*: 1dc in each st to end. (8)

Rnds 10-13: 1dc in each st to end. (8)

LEFT LEG, BODY AND HEAD

With brown yarn

Rnd 1: 6ch, 1dc in 2nd ch from hook, 3dc, 4dc in next st, work remaining sts along the other side of the chs, 3dc, 3dc in next st, join. (14)

Work in spirals in continuous rounds without joining (unless otherwise stated), moving stitch marker up each round.

Rnd 2: 3dc, [2dc in next st] 4 times, 3dc, [2dc in next st] 4 times. (22)

Rnd 3 *in blo*: 3dc, [dc2tog] 4 times, 3dc, [dc2tog] 4 times. (14)

Rnd 4: 2dc, [dc2tog] 4 times, 1dc in each st to end. (10)

Rnd 5: 2dc, [dc2tog] twice, 1dc in each st to end. (8)

Rnds 6-8: 1dc in each st to end. (8)

With grey yarn

Rnd 9 *in blo*: 1dc in each st to end. (8)

Rnds 10-13: 1dc in each st to end. (8)

Rnd 14: 4ch, and join with a sl st to right leg, 1dc around right leg, then continue dcs across chs, around left leg, and across the other side of the chs. (24)

Rnds 15-27: 1dc in each st to end. (24)

Rnd 28: [4dc, dc2tog] 4 times. (20)

Rnd 29: 1dc in each st to end. (20)

Rnd 30: [3dc, dc2tog] 4 times. (16)

Rnd 31: 1dc in each st to end. (16)

Rnd 32: [2dc, dc2tog] 4 times. (12)

With flesh yarn

Rnd 33: [1dc, dc2tog] 4 times. (8)

Rnd 34: 1dc in each to end. (8)

Rnd 35: [2dc in next st, 1dc] 4 times. (12)
Rnd 36: 2dc in each st to end. (24)
Rnds 37-40: 1dc in each st to end. (24)
Rnd 41: 1dc in each st, until you get to the middle of the face, 4htrcl in next st, 1dc in each st to end. (24)
Rnds 42-44: 1dc in each st to end. (24)
Add eyes, sew on a mouth.
Rnd 45: [dc2tog, 2dc] 6 times. (18)
Rnd 46: [dc2tog, 1dc] 6 times. (12)
Rnd 47: dc2tog until hole closes.

BOOT CUFFS
With brown yarn
Turn Macbeth upside down, and work into front loops of rnd 9 of each leg, 2ch, 1htr into each st, join with a sl st. (8)

TUNIC
With black yarn
Ch17
Row 1: 1htr in 3rd ch from hook, 1htr in each ch to end, turn. (16)
Row 2: 2ch, 2htr, 2htr in next st, [3htr, 2htr in next st] 3 times, turn. (20)
Row 3: 2ch, 3htr, 2htr in next st, [4htr, 2htr in next st] 3 times, turn. (24)
Rows 4-12: 2ch, 1htr in each st to end, turn. (24)
Wrap around figure, sew from row 4-12.
Use grey yarn to create a criss-cross at the top.

BELT
With grey yarn
Ch36
Row 1: 1htr in 3rd ch from hook, 1htr in each ch to end. (35)
Sew ends together and place around waist.

ARMS
(Make 2)
With black yarn
Rnd 1: 8dc in magic ring. (8)
Rnds 2-8: 1dc in each st to end. (8)
With light grey yarn
Rnds 9-14: 1dc in each st to end. (8)
Sew onto sides of body.

BEARD
With orange yarn
Ch16
Row 1: 1dc in 2nd ch from hook, 1dc in each ch to end, turn. (15)
Row 2: 5dc, 5ch, miss 5 sts, 5dc, turn. (15)
Rows 3-4: 1ch, 1dc in each st to end, turn. (15)
Sew onto the face.
Make hair cap (see page 125) with orange yarn and sew on head.

TARTAN
Prepare five mini balls of green, and five of red, although keep the main balls ready for rows 3-5.
Work with right side facing at all times. Fasten off the yarn at the end of the row and, with right side still facing, reattach yarn in first stitch to work next row.
With blue yarn
Ch46
Row 1: 1dc in 2nd ch from hook, 4dc, [*with green yarn, 1dc, with red yarn, 1dc, with green yarn, 1dc, with blue yarn, 5dc*] 5 times, *fasten off blue yarn.* (45)
Row 2: *Instead of turning, reattach blue yarn on the right side,* 1ch, 5dc, [*with green yarn, 1dc, with red yarn, 1dc, with green yarn, 1dc*] 5 times. (45)
Row 3: *with green yarn from the main ball,* 1ch, 6dc, [*with red yarn, 1dc, with green yarn, 7dc*] 4 times, *with red yarn, 1dc, with green yarn, 6dc.* (45)
Row 4: *with red yarn from the main ball,* 1ch, 1dc in each st to end. (45)
Row 5: rep row 3. (45)
Rows 6-7: rep row 2. (45)
Sew the ends together and place on Macbeth.

> *'Is this a dagger which I see before me, The handle toward my hand?'*
>
> Macbeth (Act I, Scene 7)

TARTAN CHART

YARN

100% cotton 4ply; light grey, black, dark grey, burgundy

SUGGESTED YARN:
'Must-have' from Yarn and Colors: Silver, Black, Shark Grey, Burgundy

OTHER MATERIALS

2.5 mm (C/2) crochet hook
Yarn needle
6 mm (1/3 in) safety eyes x 2
Stitch marker
Fibrefill stuffing

PATTERN NOTES

- Instructions are for one witch only, so you may want to make three.
- Instead of black and white around the eyes, the witches have burgundy.
- For htrcl stitch instructions, see page 124.
- The hair has been made without a hair cap and by using chains to create a bedraggled look. An example of this is shown, using green yarn so it can be seen more clearly.

Witches

RIGHT LEG

With light grey yarn
Rnd 1: 6ch, 1dc in 2nd ch from hook, 3dc, 4dc in next st, work remaining sts along the other side of the chs, 3dc, 3dc in next st, join. (14)
Work in spirals in continuous rounds without joining (unless otherwise stated), moving stitch marker up each round.
Rnd 2: 3dc, [2dc in next st] 4 times, 3dc, [2dc in next st] 4 times. (22)
Rnd 3: 3dc, [dc2tog] 4 times, 3dc, [dc2tog] 4 times. (14)
Rnd 4: 2dc, [dc2tog] 4 times, 1dc in each st to end. (10)
Rnd 5: 2dc, [dc2tog] twice, 1dc in each st to end. (8)
Rnds 6-11: 1dc in each st to end. (8)

LEFT LEG, BODY AND HEAD

With light grey yarn
Rnd 1: 6ch, 1dc in 2nd ch from hook, 3dc, 4dc in next st, work remaining sts along the other side of the chs, 3dc, 3dc in next st, join. (14)
Work in spirals in continuous rounds without joining (unless otherwise stated), moving stitch marker up each round.
Rnd 2: 3dc, [2dc in next st] 4 times, 3dc, [2dc in next st] 4 times. (22)
Rnd 3: 3dc, [dc2tog] 4 times, 3dc, [dc2tog] 4 times. (14)
Rnd 4: 2dc, [dc2tog] 4 times, 1dc in each st to end. (10)
Rnd 5: 2dc, [dc2tog] twice, 1dc in each st to end. (8)
Rnds 6-11: 1dc in each st to end. (8)
With black yarn

Rnd 12: 4ch, and join with a sl st to right leg, 1dc around right leg, then continue dcs across chs, around left leg, and across the other side of the chs. (24)

Rnds 13-16: 1dc in each st to end. (24)

With burgundy yarn

Rnd 17 *in blo:* 1dc in each st to end. (24)

With black yarn

Rnds 18-25: 1dc in each st to end. (24)

Rnd 26: [4dc, dc2tog] 4 times. (20)

Rnd 27: 1dc in each st to end. (20)

Rnd 28: [3dc, dc2tog] 4 times. (16)

Rnd 29: 1dc in each st to end. (16)

Rnd 30: [2dc, dc2tog] 4 times. (12)

With light grey yarn

Rnd 31: [1dc, dc2tog] 4 times. (8)

Rnd 32: 1dc in each st to end. (8)

Rnd 33: [2dc in next st, 1dc] 4 times. (12)

Rnd 34: 2dc in each st to end. (24)

Rnds 35-38: 1dc in each st to end. (24)

Rnd 39: 1dc in each st, until you get to the middle of the face, 5ch, 3dc in 2nd ch from hook, work dcs down remaining chs, sl st in next stitch in main round of round 38, 1dc in each st to end. (24)

Rnds 40-42: 1dc in each st to end. (24)

Attach eyes and add mouth.

Rnd 43: [dc2tog, 2dc] 6 times. (18)

Rnd 44: [dc2tog, 1dc] 6 times. (12)

Rnd 45: dc2tog until hole closes.

ARMS

(Make 2)

With light grey yarn

Rnd 1: 8dc in magic ring. (8)

Rnds 2-4: 1dc in each st to end. (8)

With black yarn

Rnds 5-14: 1dc in each st to end. (8)

Sew onto sides of body.

SKIRT

With black yarn

Turn the witch upside down and work into the front loops of round 17, join at the back.

Rnd 1: 2ch, 1htr, [2htr in next st, 2htr] 7 times, join. (30)

Rnds 2-8: 2ch, 1htr in each st to end, join. (30)

HAIR

The witches' hair is made without a hair cap, as the hair will look more straggley than the hair of the other characters.

Wrap the dark grey yarn around a book 30 times. Cut from one end, so you have 30 strands of hair.

Lay them out in twos. Chain st along the middle of the strands so that each chain holds two strands of hair.

Sew onto the head, along the chains.

Cauldron

With black yarn

Rnd 1: 8dc in magic ring. (8)

Rnd 2: 2dc in each st to end. (16)

Rnd 3: [2dc in next st, 1dc] 8 times. (24)

Rnd 4: [2dc in next st, 2dc] 8 times. (32)

Rnd 5: [2dc in next st, 3dc] 8 times. (40)

Rnd 6: [2dc in next st, 4dc] 8 times. (48)

Rnds 7-20: 1dc in each st to end. (48)

Rnd 21: 2dc in each st to end. (96)

Make two handles with 10ch, and sew these into the sides. Fill with stuffing or bubbles for a spooky look.

'Double, double, toil and trouble;
Fire burn, and cauldron bubble.'

Three Witches (Act IV, Scene 1)

A Midsummer Night's Dream

'What angel wakes me from my flow'ry bed?'

Titania (Act III, Scene 1)

Titania, the elegant fairy queen, and Nick Bottom, a weaver and part-time actor, are brought together in the woods by magic and mischief. Titania's husband, King Oberon, is annoyed by her disobedience and wants to play a trick on her. He anoints her eyes with a special juice that will make her fall in love with the next creature she sees. To add even more mischief, the fairy Puck sees some workers in the forest rehearsing a performance and decides to give Nick Bottom an ass's head. Bottom wanders into the forest, wondering why his friends have run away, begins singing and awakens Titania, who falls madly in love with him at first sight.

A Midsummer Night's Dream mixes a mystical fairyland with Athenian mortals, shows us that the course of true love never did run smooth and gives us an insight into amateur dramatics. The action of the play all takes place over one night, and its quick-moving narrative even inspired a Hollywood blockbuster. After reading the play, director John McTiernan was inspired to change the script of *Die Hard* so that the entire movie's action also took place over a single night. Diarist Samuel Pepys was not a fan however and noted in 1662, 'the most insipid, ridiculous play that I ever saw in my life.'

YARN

100% cotton 4ply in green, flesh, turquoise, fuchsia, light grey
Optional: use scrap yarn in different colours for flowers

SUGGESTED YARN:

'Must-have' from Yarn and Colors: Grass, Taupe, Petroleum, Fuchsia, Silver

MATERIALS

2.5 mm (C/2) crochet hook
Yarn needle
6 mm (1/3 in) safety eyes x 2
Stitch marker
Fibrefill stuffing
PVA glue
Greaseproof paper

PATTERN NOTES

- For hair instructions see page 125.
- For htrcl stitch instructions, see page 124.
- For further details of how to read charts see page 127.

Titania

RIGHT LEG

With green yarn

Rnd 1: 6ch, 1dc in 2nd ch from hook, 3dc, 4dc in next st, work remaining sts along the other side of the chs, 3dc, 3dc in next st, join. (14)

Work in spirals in continuous rounds without joining (unless otherwise stated), moving stitch marker up each round.

Rnd 2: 3dc, [2dc in next st] 4 times, 3dc, [2dc in next st] 4 times. (22)

Rnd 3 in blo: 3dc, [dc2tog] 4 times, 3dc, [dc2tog] 4 times. (14)

Rnd 4: 2dc, [dc2tog] 4 times, 1dc in each st to end. (10)

With flesh yarn

Rnd 5: 2dc, [dc2tog] twice, 1dc in each st to end. (8)

Rnds 6-13: 1dc in each st to end. (8)

LEFT LEG, BODY AND HEAD

With green yarn

Rnd 1: 6ch, 1dc in 2nd ch from hook, 3dc, 4dc in next st, work remaining sts along the other side of the chs, 3dc, 3dc in next st, join. (14)

Work in spirals in continuous rounds without joining (unless otherwise stated), moving stitch marker up each round.

Rnd 2: 3dc, [2dc in next st] 4 times, 3dc, [2dc in next st] 4 times. (22)

Rnd 3 in blo: 3dc, [dc2tog] 4 times, 3dc, [dc2tog] 4 times. (14)

Rnd 4: 2dc, [dc2tog] 4 times, 1dc in each st to end. (10)

With flesh yarn

Rnd 5: 2dc, [dc2tog] twice, 1dc in each st to end. (8)

Rnds 6-13: 1dc in each st to end. (8)

With turquoise yarn

Rnd 14: 4ch, and join with a sl st to right leg, 1dc around right leg, then continue dcs across chs, around left leg, and across the other side of the chs. (24)

Rnds 15-19: 1dc in each st to end. (24)

Rnd 20 in blo: 1dc in each st to end. (24)

Rnds 21-27: 1dc in each st to end. (24)

Rnd 28: [4dc, dc2tog] 4 times. (20)

Rnd 29: 1dc in each st to end. (20)

Rnd 30: [3dc, dc2tog] 4 times. (16)

With flesh yarn

Rnd 31: 1dc in each st to end. (16)

Rnd 32: [2dc, dc2tog] 4 times. (12)

Rnd 33: [1dc, dc2tog] 4 times. (8)

Rnd 34: 1dc in each st to end. (8)

Rnd 35: [2dc in next st, 1dc] 4 times. (12)

Rnd 36: 2dc in each st to end. (24)

Rnds 37-40: 1dc in each st to end. (24)

Rnd 41: 1dc in each st until you come to the middle of the face, 4htrcl in next st, 1dc in each st to end. (24)
Rnds 42-44: 1dc in each st to end. (24)
Attach eyes, sew on a little mouth
Rnd 45: [dc2tog, 2dc] 6 times. (18)
Rnd 46: [dc2tog, 1dc] 6 times. (12)
Rnd 47: dc2tog to close hole.

WAISTBAND
With green yarn
Join to front loops of round 20.
Rnd 1: 2ch, 1htr in each st, join with sl st. (18)

LEAF SKIRT
With green yarn
Instructions are for one leaf, and these are repeated across the waistband.
Row 1: 4ch, miss 1 st, sl st in next st, turn. (4)
Row 2: work in the ch-sp of previous row, 1ch, 1htr, 2tr, 2dtr, 2tr, 2htr, sl st, turn. (9).
Row 3: 1ch, 2dc, 1htr, 1ch, 1tr, 1ch, [1tr, 3ch, 1tr] in the next st, 1ch, 1tr, 1ch, 1htr, 2dc, 1sl st in the waistband. (18)

ARMS
(Make 2)
With flesh
Rnd 1: 8dc in magic ring. (8)
Rnds 2-14: 1dc in each st to end. (8)
Fasten off, leave enough yarn for sewing.

CROWN
With gold yarn
Ch36, join with sl st to form ring
Rnd 1: 2ch, 1htr in each st to end, join. (36)
Rnd 2: [3ch, 1dc in 2nd ch from hook, 1htr in next ch, miss 2 sts in row 1, sl st in next st, sl st in next st] twice.

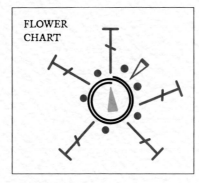

FLOWER CHART

FLOWERS
(Make as many as needed in different colours)
Rnd 1: [1tr, 1sl st] 5 times in magic ring, join. (5)
Optional, use a different colour to make a few stitches in the middle of the flower.

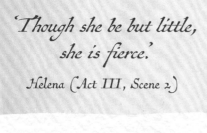

WING CHART

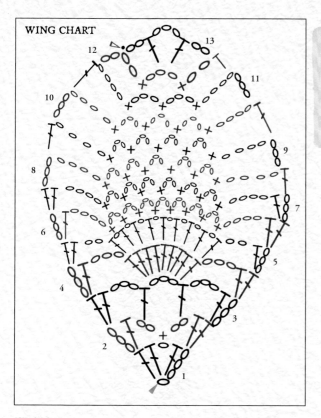

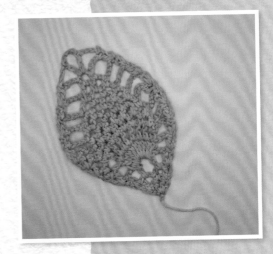

WINGS

(Make 2)

With light grey yarn

Begin your slip knot 10-15 cm along the yarn, as you'll be sewing in from this side.

4ch

Row 1: [1tr, 1ch, 2tr] in 4th ch from hook, turn. (5)

Row 2: 3ch, 1tr in next st, 2ch, 1dc in 1ch-sp, 2ch, 2tr in last st, turn. (9)

Row 3: 3ch, 1tr in next st, [3ch, 1tr in next 2ch-sp] twice, 3ch, 2tr in last st, turn. (15)

Row 4: 3ch, 1tr in next st, 3ch, 9tr in centre 3ch-sp, 3ch, 2tr in last st, turn. (19)

Row 5: 3ch, 1tr in next st, 2ch, 1tr in next tr, [1ch, 1tr] in each of next 8tr, 2ch, 2tr in last st, turn. (25)

Row 6: 3ch, 1tr in next st, 4ch, 1dc in first 1ch-sp, [3ch, 1dc in next 3ch-sp] 7 times, 4ch, 2tr in last st, turn. (41)

Row 7: 3ch, 1tr in next st, 4ch, 1dc in next 3ch-sp, [3ch, 1dc in next 3ch-sp] 6 times, 4ch, 2tr in last st, turn. (37)

Row 8: 7ch (counts as 1tr, 4ch), 1dc in first 3ch-sp, [3ch, 1dc in next 3ch-sp] 5 times, 4ch, 1tr in last st, turn. (31)

Row 9: 7ch (counts as 1tr, 4ch), 1dc in first 3ch-sp, [3ch, 1dc in next 3ch-sp] 4 times 4ch, 1tr in 3rd of 7ch, turn. (27)

Row 10: 7ch (counts as 1tr, 4ch), 1dc in first 3ch-sp, [3ch, 1dc in next 3ch-sp] 3 times, 4ch, 1tr in 3rd of 7ch, turn. (23)

Row 11: 7ch (counts as 1tr, 4ch), 1dc in first 3ch-sp, [3ch, 1dc in next 3ch-sp] twice, 4ch, 1tr in 3rd of 7ch, turn. (19)

Row 12: 4ch (counts as 1htr, 2ch), 1dc in first 3ch-sp, 3ch, 1dc in next 3ch-sp, 2ch, 1htr in 3rd of 7ch, turn. (11)

Row 13: 2ch, [1htr, 3ch, 1htr] in 3ch-sp, 2ch, sl st to 2nd of 4ch. (9)

Place the wings onto greaseproof paper, and apply the PVA glue to the wings. Leave to dry and harden overnight, and sew to the back of the Titania.

CONSTRUCTION

Make hair according to instructions on page 125, with fuchsia yarn. Sew wings onto the back.

Sew flowers onto dress at various points.

YARN

100% cotton 4ply in black, khaki, brown, white, grey
Optional: use scrap yarn in different colours for flowers

SUGGESTED YARN:
'Must-have' from Yarn and Colors: Black, Olive, Brownie, White, Titanium

MATERIALS

2.5 mm (C/2) crochet hook
Yarn needle
6 mm (1/3 in) safety eyes x 2
Stitch marker
Fibrefill stuffing

PATTERN NOTES

- For the flowers, follow the instructions in Titania's pattern (page 29) and sew them together to make a crown.
- Stuff the snout before sewing on.

Bottom

TUNIC
With brown yarn
Ch18, sl st to join
Rnd 1: 2ch, 1htr in each st to end, join. (18)
Rnd 2: 2ch, 1htr, 2htr in next st, [2htr, 2htr in next st] 5 times, join. (24)
Rnd 3: 2ch, 4htr, 2htr in next st, [5htr, 2htr in next st] 3 times, join. (28)
Rnds 4-10: 2ch, 1htr in each st to end, join. (28)
Use black yarn to create 'X' stitches across the bottom.

SNOUT
With white yarn
Rnd 1: 6dc in magic ring. (6)
Rnd 2: 2dc in each st to end. (12)
Rnds 3-4: 1dc in each st to end. (12)
With grey yarn
Rnds 5-7: 1dc in each st to end. (12)
Use black yarn to embroider on nostrils and mouth.

RIGHT LEG
With black yarn
Rnd 1: 6ch, 1dc in 2nd ch from hook, 3dc, 4dc in next st, work remaining sts along the other side of the chs, 3dc, 3dc in next st, join. (14)
Work in spirals in continuous rounds without joining (unless otherwise stated), moving stitch marker up each round.
Rnd 2: 3dc, [2dc in next st] 4 times, 3dc, [2dc in next st] 4 times. (22)
Rnd 3 *in blo*: 3dc, [dc2tog] 4 times, 3dc, [dc2tog] 4 times. (14)
Rnd 4: 2dc, [dc2tog] 4 times, 1dc in each st to end. (10)
Rnd 5: 2dc, [dc2tog]twice, 1dc in each st to end. (8)
Rnds 6-8: 1dc in each st to end. (8)
With khaki yarn
Rnds 9-13: 1dc in each st to end. (8)

LEFT LEG, BODY AND HEAD

With black yarn

Rnd 1: 6ch, 1dc in 2nd ch from hook, 3dc, 4dc in next st, work remaining sts along the other side of the chs, 3dc, 3dc in next st, join. (14)

Work in spirals in continuous rounds without joining (unless otherwise stated), moving stitch marker up each round.

Rnd 2: 3dc, [2dc in next st] 4 times, 3dc, [2dc in next st] 4 times. (22)

Rnd 3 in blo: 3dc, [dc2tog] 4 times, 3dc, [dc2tog] 4 times. (14)

Rnd 4: 2dc, [dc2tog] 4 times, 1dc in each st to end. (10)

Rnd 5: 2dc, [dc2tog] twice, 1dc in each st to end. (8)

Rnds 6-8: 1dc in each st to end. (8)

With khaki yarn

Rnds 9-13: 1dc in each st to end. (8)

Rnd 14: 4ch, and join with a sl st to right leg, 1dc around right leg, then continue dcs across chs, around left leg, and across the other side of the chs. (24)

Rnds 15-27: 1dc in each st to end. (24)

Rnd 28: [4dc, dc2tog] 4 times. (20)

Rnd 29: 1dc in each st to end. (20)

Rnd 30: [3dc, dc2tog] 4 times. (16)

Rnd 31: 1dc in each st to end. (16)

With grey yarn

Rnd 32: [2dc, dc2tog] 4 times. (12)

Rnd 33: [1dc, dc2tog] 4 times. (8)

Rnd 34: 1dc in each st to end. (8)

Add tunic

Rnd 35: [2dc in st, 1dc] 4 times. (12)

Rnd 36: 2dc in next st to end. (24)

Rnds 37-45: 1dc in each st to end. (24)

Attach snout and eyes.

Rnd 46: [dc2tog, 2dc] 6 times. (18)

Rnd 47: [dc2tog, 1dc] 6 times. (12)

Rnd 48: dc2tog until hole closes.

EARS

(Make 2)

With grey yarn

Rnd 1: 4dc in magic ring. (4)

Rnd 2: 1dc in each st to end. (4)

Rnd 3: [2dc in next st, 1dc] twice. (6)

Rnd 4: 1dc in each st to end. (6)

Rnd 5: [2dc in next st, 1dc] 3 times. (9)

Rnds 6-10: 1dc in each st to end. (9)

ARMS

(Make 2)

With flesh yarn

Rnd 1: 8dc in magic ring. (8)

Rnds 2-4: 1dc in each st to end. (8)

With white yarn

Rnds 5-14: 1dc in each st to end. (8)

FLOWERS

(Make as many as needed in different colours)

Rnd 1: [1tr, 1sl st] 5 times in magic ring, join. (5)

Optional, use a different colour for the middle.

CONSTRUCTION

Sew ears to head and sew arms to side of body. Sew flowers together to make a crown.

'I have had a most rare vision. I had a dream, past the wit of man to say what dream it was... The eye of man hath not heard, the ear of man hath not seen, man's hand is not able to taste, his tongue to conceive, nor his heart to report, what my dream was.'

Bottom (Act IV, Scene 1)

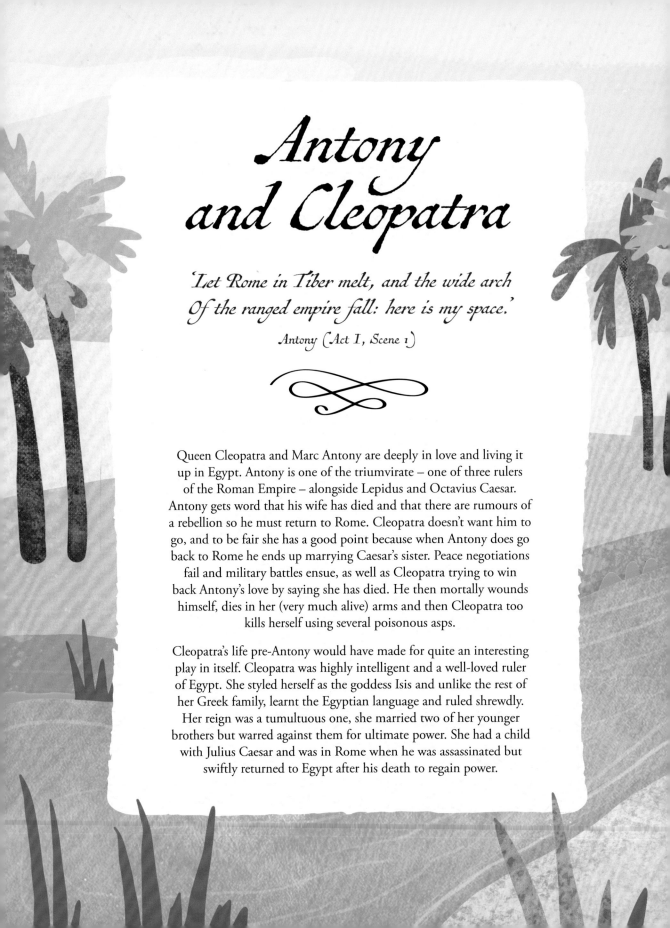

Antony and Cleopatra

*'Let Rome in Tiber melt, and the wide arch
Of the ranged empire fall: here is my space.'*

Antony (Act I, Scene 1)

Queen Cleopatra and Marc Antony are deeply in love and living it up in Egypt. Antony is one of the triumvirate – one of three rulers of the Roman Empire – alongside Lepidus and Octavius Caesar. Antony gets word that his wife has died and that there are rumours of a rebellion so he must return to Rome. Cleopatra doesn't want him to go, and to be fair she has a good point because when Antony does go back to Rome he ends up marrying Caesar's sister. Peace negotiations fail and military battles ensue, as well as Cleopatra trying to win back Antony's love by saying she has died. He then mortally wounds himself, dies in her (very much alive) arms and then Cleopatra too kills herself using several poisonous asps.

Cleopatra's life pre-Antony would have made for quite an interesting play in itself. Cleopatra was highly intelligent and a well-loved ruler of Egypt. She styled herself as the goddess Isis and unlike the rest of her Greek family, learnt the Egyptian language and ruled shrewdly. Her reign was a tumultuous one, she married two of her younger brothers but warred against them for ultimate power. She had a child with Julius Caesar and was in Rome when he was assassinated but swiftly returned to Egypt after his death to regain power.

YARN

100% cotton 4ply in brown, light brown, flesh, burgundy, bronze

SUGGESTED YARN:
'Must-have' from Yarn and Colors: Brownie, Cigar, Peach, Burgundy, Gold

OTHER MATERIALS

2.5 mm (C/2) crochet hook
Yarn needle
6 mm (1/3 in) safety eyes x 2
Stitch marker
Fibrefill stuffing

PATTERN NOTES

- For htrcl stitch instructions, see page 124.
- For hair instructions, see page 125.

Antony

TUNIC
With brown yarn
Ch18 *join with sl st*
Rnd 1: 2ch, [2htr in next st, 1htr] 8 times, 2htr in next st, join. (27)
Rnds 2-7: 2ch, 1htr in each st to end, join. (27)
Don't fasten off brown.
With burgundy yarn
Rnd 8 *in blo*: 2ch, 1htr in each st to end, join. (27)
Rnds 9-13: 2ch, 1htr in each st to end, join. (27)
Fasten off burgundy yarn.
Work with brown yarn into front loops of rnd 7.
Rnd 14: [8ch, 1htr in 3rd ch from hook, 1htr in each of the remaining chs, miss 2 sts in rnd 7, sl st] 9 times.
Fasten off. Embroider chain stitches with bronze.

EMBELLISHMENT
With bronze yarn
Rnd 1: 3ch, 7htr in first ch, join. (8)
Sew onto the front of the tunic.

CAPE
With burgundy yarn
Ch13
Row 1: 1htr in 3rd ch from hook, 1htr in each st to end, turn. (12)
Row 2: 2ch, 2htr in next st [1htr, 2htr in next st] 5 times, turn. (18)
Rows 3-11: 2ch, 1htr in each st to end, turn. (18)

SHOULDER PIECES
(Make 2)
With bronze yarn
Rnd 1: 2ch, 5dc in first ch, join. (6)
Sew the cape onto the back of the uniform, and sew the two shoulder pieces.

BELT
With bronze yarn
Ch36 join with sl st.

RIGHT LEG
With brown yarn
Rnd 1: 6ch, 1dc in 2nd ch from hook, 3dc, 4dc in next st, work remaining sts along the other side of the chs, 3dc, 3dc in next st, join. (14)

Work in spirals in continuous rounds without joining (unless otherwise stated), moving stitch marker up each round.

Rnd 2: 3dc, [2dc in next st] 4 times, 3dc, [2dc in next st] 4 times. (22)

With flesh yarn

Rnd 3 in blo: 3dc, [dc2tog] 4 times, 3dc, [dc2tog] 4 times. (14)

Rnd 4: 2dc, [dc2tog] 4 times, 1dc in each st to end. (10)

Rnd 5: 2dc, [dc2tog] twice, 1dc to in each st to end. (8)

Rnds 6-13: 1dc in each st to end. (8)

LEFT LEG, BODY AND HEAD

With brown yarn

Rnd 1: 6ch, 1dc in 2nd ch from hook, 3dc, 4dc in next st, work remaining sts along the other side of the chs, 3dc, 3dc in next st, join. (14)

Work in spirals in continuous rounds without joining (unless otherwise stated), moving stitch marker up each round.

Rnd 2: 3dc, [2dc in next st] 4 times, 3dc, [2dc in next st] 4 times. (22)

With flesh yarn

Rnd 3 in blo: 3dc, [dc2tog] 4 times, 3dc, [dc2tog] 4 times. (14)

Rnd 4: 2dc, [dc2tog] 4 times, 1dc in each st to end. (10)

Rnd 5: 2dc, [dc2tog] twice, 1dc in each st to end. (8)

Rnds 6-7: 1dc in each st to end. (8)

Rnds 8 in blo: 1dc in each st to end. (8)

Rnds 9-13: 1dc in each st to end. (8)

Rnd 14: 4ch, and join with a sl st to right leg, 1dc around right leg, then continue dcs across chs, around left leg, and across the other side of the chs. (24)

Rnds 15-27: 1dc in each st to end. (24)

Rnd 28: [4dc, dc2tog] 4 times. (20)

Rnd 29: 1dc in each st to end. (20)

Rnd 30: [3dc, dc2tog] 4 times. (16)

Rnd 31: 1dc in each st to end. (16)

Rnd 32: [2dc, dc2tog] 4 times. (12)

Rnd 33: [1dc, dc2tog] 4 times. (8)

Rnd 34: 1dc in each st to end. (8)

Put tunic on the figure and add the belt.

Rnd 35: [2dc in next st, 1dc] 4 times. (12)

Rnd 36: 2dc in next st to end. (24)

Rnds 37-40: 1dc in each st to end. (24)

Rnd 41: 1dc in each st until you get to the middle of the face, 4htrcl in next st, 1dc in each st to end. (24)

Rnds 42-44: 1dc in each st to end. (24)

Attach eyes and sew on mouth.

Rnd 45: [dc2tog, 2dc] 6 times. (18)

Rnd 46: [dc2tog, 1dc] 6 times. (12)

Rnd 47: dc2tog until hole closes.

ARMS

(Make 2)

With flesh yarn

Rnd 1: 8dc in magic ring. (8)

Rnds 2-9: 1dc in each st to end. (8)

With burgundy yarn

Rnds 10-14: 1dc in each st to end. (8)

Sew arms onto sides of body

SANDALS

(Make 2)

With brown yarn

Ch46

Fold in half. Thread 30 cm of brown yarn onto your needle. Count three sets of stitches up from the fold, and sew these together down to the fold. Place on top of the foot and sew to the front. Work stitches along to secure to foot. Use your hook to hide the end of the thread. Bring chains around the back of the foot to make a cross, then do the same at the front. Cross again at the back if you have any left, and loosely sew on to secure. Weave in any loose ends.

Make hair cap (see page 125) with light brown yarn and sew onto head.

'There's beggary in the love that can be reckoned.'

Antony (Act I, Scene 1)

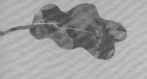

YARN

100% cotton 4ply in brown, flesh, white, gold, black, blue, green, red, black

SUGGESTED YARN:
'Must-have' from Yarn and Colors:
Brownie, Limestone, White, Mustard, Black, Turquoise, Peony Leaf, Pepper

OTHER MATERIALS

2.5 mm (C/2) crochet hook
Yarn needle
6 mm (1/3 in) safety eyes x 2
Stitch marker
Fibrefill stuffing

PATTERN NOTES

- Cleopatra will only need scrap amounts of red, blue and green.
- For htrcl stitch instructions, see page 124.

Cleopatra

DRESS

With white yarn
Ch18, join with sl st to make a ring.
Rnd 1: 2ch, [2htr in next st, 1htr] 8 times, 2htr in next st, join. (27)
Rnds 2-7: 2ch, 1htr in each st to end, join. (27)
With gold yarn
Rnd 8: 2ch, 1htr in each st to end, join. (27)
With white yarn
Rnds 9-13: 2ch, 1htr in each st to end, join. (27)

DRESS FRONTPIECE

With gold yarn
Ch5
Rnd 1: 1htr in 3rd ch from hook, 1htr in each st to end. (4)
Rnds 2-5: 2ch, 1htr in each st to end. (4)
Fasten off, sew to front of dress at the belt.

NECKPIECE

With gold yarn
Ch16, join with sl st to make a ring
Rnd 1: 1ch, [1dc, 2dc in next st] 8 times, join. (24)
With blue yarn
Rnd 2: 1ch, [2dc in next st, 2dc] 8 times, join. (32)
Fasten off blue yarn
With gold yarn
Rnd 3: 1ch, 1dc in each st to end, join. (32)
Rnd 4: 1ch, 2dc, [*with green yarn*, 2htrcl, *with gold yarn*, 3dc] 4 times, *with red yarn*, 3htrcl, *with gold yarn*, 3dc, [*with green yarn*, 2htrcl, *with gold yarn*, 3dc] twice, *with green yarn*, 2htrcl, *with gold yarn*, 1dc, join. (32)
Rnd 5: 1ch, 1dc in each st to end, join. (32)

RIGHT LEG

With brown yarn

Rnd 1: 6ch, 1dc in 2nd ch from hook, 3dc, 4dc in next st, work remaining sts along the other side of the chs, 3dc, 3dc in next st, join. (14)

Work in spirals in continuous rounds without joining (unless otherwise stated), moving stitch marker up each round.

Rnd 2: 3dc, [2dc in next st] 4 times, 3dc, [2dc in next st] 4 times, sl st, 8ch to create the sandal strap. (22)

Fasten off brown yarn.

With flesh yarn

Rnd 3 *in blo*: 3dc, [dc2tog] 4 times, 3dc, [dc2tog] 4 times. (14)

Rnd 4: 2dc, [dc2tog] 4 times, 1dc in each st to end. (10)

Rnd 5: 2dc, [dc2tog] twice, 1dc in each st to end. (8)

Rnd 6: 1dc in each st to end. (8)

Place sandal strap across foot, weave end in and fasten inside.

Rnds 7-13: 1dc in each st to end. (8)

LEFT LEG, BODY AND HEAD

With brown yarn

Rnd 1: 6ch, 1dc in 2nd ch from hook, 3dc, 4dc in next st, work remaining sts along the other side of the chs, 3dc, 3dc in next st, join. (14)

Work in spirals in continuous rounds without joining (unless otherwise stated), moving stitch marker up each round.

Rnd 2: 3dc, [2dc in next st] 4 times, 3dc, [2dc in next st] 4 times, sl st, 8ch to create the sandal strap. (22)

Fasten off brown yarn.

With flesh yarn

Rnd 3 *in blo*: 3dc, [dc2tog] 4 times, 3dc, [dc2tog] 4 times. (14)

Rnd 4: 2dc, [dc2tog] 4 times, 1dc in each st to end. (10)

Rnd 5: 2dc, [dc2tog] twice, 1dc in each st to end. (8)

Rnd 6: 1dc in each st to end. (8)

Place sandal strap across foot, weave end in and fasten inside.

Rnds 7-13: 1dc in each st to end. (8)

Rnd 14: 4ch, and join with a sl st to right leg, 1dc around right leg, then continue dcs across chs, around left leg, and across the other side of the chs. (24)

Rnds 15-27: 1dc in each st to end. (24)

Rnd 28: [4dc, dc2tog] 4 times. (20)

Rnd 29: 1dc in each st to end. (20)

Rnd 30: [3dc, dc2tog] 4 times. (16)

Rnd 31: 1dc in each st to end. (16)

Rnd 32: [2dc, dc2tog] 4 times. (12)

Rnd 33: [1dc, dc2tog] 4 times. (8)

Rnd 34: 1dc in each st to end. (8)

Add dress and neckpiece.

Rnd 35: [2dc in next st, 1dc] 4 times. (12)

Rnd 36: 2dc in each st to end. (24)

Rnds 37-40: 1dc in each st to end. (24)

Rnd 41: 1dc in each st until you get to the middle of the face, 4htrcl in next st, 1dc in each st to end. (24)

Rnds 42-44: 1dc in each st to end. (24)

Add eyes, eyebrows and eyeshadow (with blue) and sew on a mouth with red.

Rnd 45: [dc2tog, 2dc] 6 times. (18)

Rnd 46: [dc2tog, 1dc] 6 times. (12)

Rnd 47: dc2tog until hole closes.

> *'Age cannot wither her, nor custom stale her infinite variety.'*
>
> Enobarbus (Act II, Scene 2)

ARMS

(Make 2)

With flesh yarn

Rnd 1: 8dc in magic ring. (8)

Rnds 2-14: 1dc in each st to end. (8)

Sew onto sides of body.

BRACELET

(Make 2)

With gold yarn

Ch12, join

Rnd 1: 1ch, 1dc in each st to end, join. (12)

Rnd 2: 1dc, [*with blue yarn*, 1dc, *with gold yarn*, 3dc] twice, *with blue yarn*, 1dc, *with gold yarn*, 2dc, join.(12)

Rnd 3: 1ch, 1dc in each st to end, join. (12)

Place bracelets around arms.

HAIR

With black yarn

Rnd 1: 6dc in magic ring. (6)

Rnd 2: 2dc in each st to end. (12)

Rnd 3: [2dc in next st, 1dc] 6 times. (18)

Rnd 4: [2dc in next st, 2dc] 6 times. (24)

Rnds 5-7: 1dc in each st to end. (24)

Rnd 8: [10ch, work 1dc in 2nd ch from hook, and continue with 1dc along the rest of the chs, sl st in rnd 7] twice.

Sew hair onto head.

HEADDRESS

Piece 1

With gold yarn

Ch34, join

Rnd 1: 1dc in each st to end, join. (34)

Fasten off.

Piece 2

With gold yarn

Ch8

Rnd 1: 1dc in 2nd ch from hook. (8)

Fasten off, leaving a tail and use tail to sew on to piece 1. Sew the headdress onto the head if you want to keep it in place.

'*Eternity was in our lips and in our eyes.*'

Cleopatra (Act I, Scene 3)

Hamlet

'Something is rotten in the state of Denmark.'

Marcellus (Act I, Scene 4)

Things aren't going well for Prince Hamlet. His father has died and his widowed mother Gertrude has married his uncle Claudius, and Claudius is now King. Hamlet is even more annoyed when he finds out from his dad's ghost that it was actually Claudius who murdered him. He turns on Ophelia, who loves him and who he once loved, and tells her to get to a nunnery. Hamlet is intent on vengeance, fakes madness and inadvertently ends up killing Ophelia's dad (although to be fair, he shouldn't have been eavesdropping behind a tapestry). It's not the only death in this Danish tragedy; Ophelia drowns herself, Gertrude drinks poison by mistake, Hamlet kills Claudius and Ophelia's brother and eventually dies himself from his wounds. Hamlet's friend Horatio tries to kill himself – but Hamlet wants him to stay alive to tell his story.

The Tragedy of Hamlet, Prince of Denmark, is Shakespeare's longest play with 4,000 lines, and the unedited version would take around four hours to perform. One of the most famous scenes is when Hamlet finds the exhumed skull of Yorick, the old jester who entertained him as a boy. When Polish composer André Tchaikovsky died in 1982, he left his skull to the Royal Shakespeare Company, in the hope it would be used on stage for this scene, and it was! The play popularised some of the phrases we still use today including 'cruel to be kind', 'neither a borrower nor a lender be' and 'hoist with his own petard'. Sadly, there are lines in there that never really stood the test of time – 'Take you me for a sponge?'– perhaps that's one that we can bring back?

YARN

100% cotton 4ply in white, flesh, black, gold, yellow, maroon, grey

SUGGESTED YARN:
'Must-have' from Yarn and Colors: White, Peach, Black, Mustard, Golden Glow, Shark Grey

YORICK'S SKULL

100% 4 ply cotton in white, black

SUGGESTED YARN:
'Must-have' from Yarn and Colors: White, Black

OTHER MATERIALS

2.5 mm (C/2) crochet hook
Yarn needle
6 mm (1/3 in) safety eyes x 2
Stitch marker
Fibrefill stuffing

PATTERN NOTES

- For ls instructions, see page 124.
- For htrcl stitch instructions, see page 124.

Hamlet

RIGHT LEG
With black yarn
Rnd 1: 6ch, 1dc in 2nd ch from hook, 3dc, 4dc in next st, work remaining sts along the other side of the chs, 3dc, 3dc in next st, join. (14)
Work in spirals in continuous rounds without joining (unless otherwise stated), moving stitch marker up each round.
Rnd 2: 3dc, [2dc in next st] 4 times, 3dc, [2dc in next st] 4 times. (22)
Rnd 3 *in blo*: 3dc, [dc2tog] 4 times, 3dc, [dc2tog] 4 times. (14)
Rnd 4: 2dc, [dc2tog] 4 times, 1dc in each st to end. (10)
With grey yarn
Rnd 5: 2dc, [dc2tog] twice, 1dc in each st to end. (8)
Rnds 6-13: 1dc in each st to end. (8)

LEFT LEG, BODY AND HEAD
With black yarn
Rnd 1: 6ch, 1dc in 2nd ch from hook, 3dc, 4dc in next st, work remaining sts along the other side of the chs, 3dc, 3dc in next st, join. (14)
Work in spirals in continuous rounds without joining (unless otherwise stated), moving stitch marker up each round.
Rnd 2: 3dc, [2dc in next st] 4 times, 3dc, [2dc in next st] 4 times. (22)

Rnd 3 *in blo*: 3dc, [dc2tog] 4 times, 3dc, [dc2tog] 4 times. (14)
Rnd 4: 2dc, [dc2tog] 4 times, 1dc in each st to end. (10)
With grey yarn
Rnd 5: 2dc, [dc2tog] twice, 1dc in each st to end. (8)
Rnds 6-13: 1dc in each st to end. (8)
Rnd 14: 4ch, and join with a sl st to right leg, 1dc around right leg, then continue dcs across chs, around left leg, and across the other side of the chs. (24)
Rnds 15-19: 1dc in each st to end. (24)
With white yarn
Rnds 20-27: 1dc in each st to end. (24)
Rnd 28: [4dc, dc2tog] 4 times. (20)
Rnd 29: 1dc in each st to end. (20)
Rnd 30: [3dc, dc2tog] 4 times. (16)
Rnd 31: 1dc in each st to end. (16)
Rnd 32: [2dc, dc2tog] 4 times. (12)
With flesh yarn
Rnd 33: [1dc, dc2tog] 4 times. (8)
Rnd 34: 1dc in each st to end. (8)
Rnd 35: [2dc in st, 1dc] 4 times. (12)
Rnd 36: 2dc in each st to end. (24)
Rnds 37-40: 1dc in each st to end. (24)
Rnd 41: 1dc in each st until you get to the middle of face, 4htrcl in next st, 1dc in each st to end. (24)
Rnds 42-44: 1dc in each st to end. (24)
Attach eyes and sew on mouth.

Rnd 45: [dc2tog, 2dc] 6 times. (18)
Rnd 46: [dc2tog, 1dc] 6 times. (12)
Rnd 47: dc2tog until hole closes.

JACKET

With white yarn
Ch18
Row 1: 1htr in 3rd ch from hook, 14htr, 2htr in last st. (18)
Fasten off. Turn, and work into the bottom of the sts.
With black yarn
Row 2: 1ch, 1dc in next st, 2dc, 2dc in next st, [3dc, 2dc in next st] 3 times, turn. (20)
Rows 3-8: 1ch, 1dc in each st to end, turn. (20)
Row 9: 1ch, 4dc, 2dc in next st, [4dc, 2dc in next st] 3 times, turn. (24)
Rows 10-12: 1ch, 1dc in each st to end, turn. (24)
Row 13: 1ch, [5dc, 2dc in next st] 4 times, turn. (28)
Rows 14-19: 1ch, 1dc in each st to end, turn. (28)

JACKET BORDER

With gold yarn
Row 1: Begin on the side of row 2, 1ch, 2dc, 1htr (spike into the work), 2dc, 1htr, continue until corner, 3dc into corner, 2dc, 1htr, work this pattern all the way round the jacket, with 3dc into the corners.
Fasten off the yarn and rejoin at the start of the row 1 again.
Row 2: 2ch, 1htr in each st all the way around the jacket, with 3htr into the corners.
Wrap around body and sew.

ARMS

(Make 2)
With flesh yarn
Rnd 1: 8dc in magic ring. (8)
Rnds 2-4: 1dc in each st to end. (8)
With gold yarn
Rnds 5-6: 1dc in each st to end. (8)
With black yarn
Rnds 7-14: 1dc in each st to end. (8)
Attach to sides of body.

HAIR

With yellow yarn
Rnd 1: 6dc in magic ring. (6)
Rnd 2: 2ls in each st to end. (12)
Rnd 3: [2ls in next st, 1ls] 6 times. (18)
Rnd 4: [2ls in next st, 2ls] 6 times. (24)
Rnds 5-6: 1ls in each st to end. (24)
Attach to head.

SASH

With maroon yarn
Ch4
Row 1: 1dc in 2nd st from hook, 2dc, turn. (3)
Rows 2-52: 1ch, 3dc, turn. (3)
Sew ends together and place around Hamlet.

Yorick's Skull

With white yarn
Rnd 1: 6dc in magic ring. (6)
Rnd 2: 2dc in each st to end. (12)
Rnd 3: [2dc in next st, 1dc] 6 times. (18)
Rnds 4-8: 1dc in each st to end. (18)
With black yarn, embroider eye holes and nostrils.
With white yarn
Rnd 9: [dc2tog] 9 times. (9)
Rnds 10-11: 1dc in each st to end. (9)
Rnd 12 in blo: [dc2tog] 3 times until hole closes.
Use black yarn to sew on some lines to create teeth.

'Alas, poor Yorick! I knew him, Horatio:
A fellow of infinite jest.'
Hamlet (Act V, Scene 1)

45

YARN

100% cotton 4ply in light grey, grey

SUGGESTED YARN:

'Must-have' from Yarn and Colors: Silver, Shark Grey

OTHER MATERIALS

2.5 mm (C/2) crochet hook
Yarn needle
6 mm (1/3 in) safety eyes x 2
Stitch marker
Fibrefill stuffing

PATTERN NOTES

- For htrcl stitch instructions, see page 124.
- You may want to paint the Ghost's eyes with grey nail varnish just to add to the spooky look.
- For further details of how to read charts see page 127.

The Ghost

BEARD

With grey yarn
Ch16
Row 1: 1dc in 2nd ch from hook, 1dc in each st to end, turn. (15)
Row 2: 5dc, 5ch, miss 5 sts, 5dc, turn. (15)
Rows 3-4: 1ch, 1dc in each st to end, turn. (15)

RIGHT LEG

With grey yarn
Rnd 1: 6ch, 1dc in 2nd ch from hook, 3dc, 4dc in next st, work remaining sts along the other side of the chs, 3dc, 3dc in next st, join. (14)
Work in spirals in continuous rounds without joining (unless otherwise stated), moving stitch marker up each round.
Rnd 2: 3dc, [2dc in next st] 4 times, 3dc, [2dc in next st] 4 times. (22)
Rnd 3 *in blo:* 3dc, [dc2tog] 4 times, 3dc, [dc2tog] 4 times. (14)
Rnd 4: 2dc, [dc2tog] 4 times, 1dc in each st to end. (10)
Rnd 5: 2dc, [dc2tog] twice, 1dc in each st to end. (8)
Rnd 6: 1dc in each st to end. (8)
With light grey yarn
Rnds 7-13: 1dc in each st to end. (8)

LEFT LEG, BODY AND HEAD

With grey yarn
Rnd 1: 6ch, 1dc in 2nd ch from hook, 3dc, 4dc in next st, work remaining sts along the other side of the chs, 3dc, 3dc in next st, join. (14)
Work in spirals in continuous rounds without joining (unless otherwise stated), moving stitch marker up each round.
Rnd 2: 3dc, [2dc in next st] 4 times, 3dc, [2dc in next st] 4 times. (22)
Rnd 3 *in blo:* 3dc, dc2tog 4 times, 3dc, [dc2tog] 4 times. (14)
Rnd 4: 2dc, [dc2tog] 4 times, 1dc in each st to end. (10)
Rnd 5: 2dc, [dc2tog] twice, 1dc in each st to end. (8)
Rnd 6: 1dc in each st to end. (8)
With light grey yarn
Rnds 7-13: 1dc in each st to end. (8)
Rnd 14: 4ch, and join with a sl st to right leg, 1dc around right leg, then continue dcs across chs, around left leg, and across the other side of the chs. (24)
Rnds 15-27: 1dc in each st to end. (24)
Rnd 28: [4dc, dc2tog] 4 times. (20)
Rnd 29: 1dc in each st to end. (20)
Rnd 30: [3dc, dc2tog] 4 times. (16)
Rnd 31: 1dc in each st to end. (16)

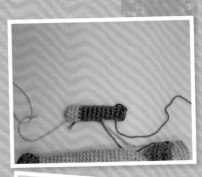

Rnd 32: [2dc, dc2tog] 4 times. (12)
Rnd 33: [1dc, dc2tog] 4 times. (8)
Rnd 34: 1dc in each st to end. (8)
Rnd 35: [2dc in next st, 1dc] 4 times. (12)
Rnd 36: 2dc in each st to end. (24)
Rnds 37-40: 1dc in each st to end. (24)
Rnd 41: 1dc in each st until you get to the middle of the face, 4htrcl in next st, 1dc in each st to end. (24)
Rnds 42-44: 1dc in each st to end. (24)
Attach eyes and sew on beard.
Rnd 45: [dc2tog, 2dc] 6 times. (24)
Rnd 46: [dc2tog, 1dc] 6 times. (18)
Rnd 47: dc2tog to close hole.

JACKET

With light grey yarn
Ch18
Row 1: 1htr in 3rd ch from hook, 14htr, 2htr in final st. (18)
Turn, and work into the bottom of the sts.
With grey yarn
Row 2: 1ch, 1dc in next st, 2dc, 2dc in next st, [3dc, 2dc in next st] 3 times, turn. (20)

Rows 3-8: 1dc in each st to end, turn. (20)
Row 9: 1ch, [4dc, 2dc in next st] 4 times, turn. (24)
Rows 10-12: 1dc in each st to end, turn. (24)
Row 13: 1ch, [5dc, 2dc in next st] 4 times, turn. (28)
Rows 14-28: 1ch, 1dc in each st to end, turn. (28)

JACKET BORDER

With light grey yarn
Begin on the side of row 2, 1ch, 2dc, 1htr (spike into the work), 2dc, 1htr, continue until corner, 3dc into corner, 2dc, 1htr, work this pattern all the way round the jacket, with 3dc into the corner.
Wrap jacket around the body, and sew up the middle.

ARMS

(Make 2)
With light grey yarn
Rnd 1: 8dc in magic ring. (8)
Rnds 2-4: 1dc in each st to end. (8)
With grey yarn
Rnds 5-14: 1dc in each st to end. (8)
Sew onto sides of body.

CROWN CHART

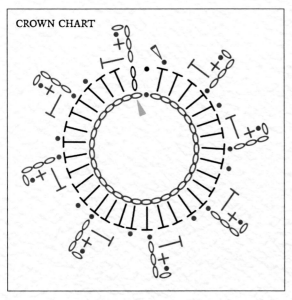

CROWN

With grey yarn
Ch32, join.
Rnd 1: 2ch, 1htr in each st, join. (32)
Rnd 2: [4ch, working down the chains, sl st in 2nd ch from hook, 1dc, 1htr, miss 2sts in rnd 1, sl st in the next 2 sts of rnd 1] 8 times.

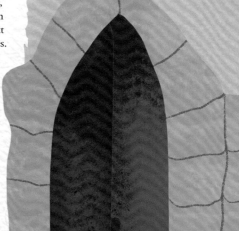

Henry VIII

'Love thyself last: cherish those hearts that hate thee:
Corruption wins not more than honesty.'

Cardinal Wolsey (Act III, Scene 2)

The King's advisor, Cardinal Wolsey, is seen by other members of court as power-hungry and ruthless, and there are suspicions that he has used his influence to have a duke arrested for treason.

Later, King Henry meets Anne Bullen (Boleyn) at a party and falls for her, which means that he has to either get his marriage annulled or get divorced. Poor Queen Katharine is out, Anne is in. Henry finds out that Wolsey wrote to the Pope opposing the marriage and he is put to death. The play ends with Princess Elizabeth's baptism and a prophecy that she will become great.

The play is thought to have been written in collaboration with John Fletcher, and is seen as a rather whitewashed portrayal of one of England's most infamous monarchs, which given Shakespeare's association with Queen Elizabeth I is not very surprising. The performance of the play itself has a notorious history. In 1613 at the Globe Theatre, a cannon was set off, misfired and set alight the incredibly flammable wooden beams and thatched roof. Within two hours the building was destroyed. According to the letters of writer Sir Henry Wotton, no one was hurt except a man whose burning breeches were put out with a bottle of ale.

YARN

100% cotton 4ply in white, grey, flesh, black, gold, orange, burgundy
100% acrylic chunky yarn in white

SUGGESTED YARN:

'Must-have' from Yarn and Colors: White, Peach, Black, Mustard, Bronze, Red Wine
James C Brett Flutterby Chunky: White

OTHER MATERIALS

2.5 mm (C/2) crochet hook
3 mm hook (D/3) crochet hook
Yarn needle
6 mm (1/3 in) safety eyes x 2
Stitch marker
Fibrefill stuffing

PATTERN NOTES

- Use 2.5 mm hook for all the 4ply yarn, use the 3 mm hook when using the white chunky yarn.
- For htrcl stitch instructions, see page 124.

Henry VIII

BEARD

With orange yarn
Ch16
Row 1: 1dc in 2nd ch from hook, 1dc to end, turn. (15)
Row 2: 1ch, 5dc, 5ch, miss 5 chs, 5dc, turn. (15)
Rows 3-4: 1ch, 1dc in each st to end, turn. (15)

RIGHT LEG

With gold yarn
Rnd 1: 6ch, 1dc in 2nd ch from hook, 3dc, 4dc in next st, work remaining sts along the other side of the chs, 3dc, 3dc in next st, join. (14)
Work in spirals in continuous rounds without joining (unless otherwise stated), moving stitch marker up each round.
Rnd 2: 3dc, [2dc in next st] 4 times, 3dc, [2dc in next st] 4 times. (22)
Rnd 3 *in blo*: 3dc, [dc2tog] 4 times, 3dc, [dc2tog] 4 times. (14)
Rnd 4: 2dc, [dc2tog] 4 times, 1dc in each st to end. (10)
With white yarn
Rnd 5: 2dc, [dc2tog] twice, 1dc in each st to end. (8)
Rnds 6-13: 1dc in each st to end. (8)

LEFT LEG, BODY AND HEAD

With gold yarn
Rnd 1: 6ch, 1dc in 2nd ch from hook, 3dc, 4dc in next st, work remaining sts along the other side of the chs, 3dc, 3dc in next st, join. (14)
Work in spirals in continuous rounds without joining (unless otherwise stated), moving stitch marker up each round.
Rnd 2: 3dc, [2dc in next st] 4 times, 3dc, [2dc in next st] 4 times. (22)
Rnd 3: in blo, 3dc, [dc2tog] 4 times, 3dc, [dc2tog] 4 times. (14)
Rnd 4: 2dc, [dc2tog] 4 times, 1dc in each st to end. (10)
With white yarn
Rnd 5: 2dc, [dc2tog] twice, 1dc in each st to end. (8)
Rnds 6-13: 1dc in each st to end. (8)
Rnd 14: 4ch, and join with a sl st to right leg, 1dc around right leg, then continue dcs across chs, around left leg, and across the other side of the chs. (24)
Rnd 15: 1dc in each st to end. (24)
Rnd 16: [2dc in next st] twice, 16dc, [2dc in next st] 3 times, 2dc, 2dc in next st. (30)
Rnd 17: 1dc, [2dc in next st, 1dc] twice

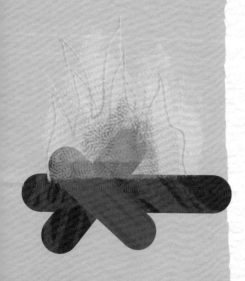

15dc, [2dc in next st, 1dc] three times, 3dc, 2dc in last st. (36)

Rnds 18-26: 1dc in each st to end. (36)

Rnd 27: [dc2tog, 4dc] 7 times. (32)

Rnd 28: 1dc in each st to end. (32)

Rnd 29: [dc2tog, 2dc] 8 times. (24)

Rnds 30-33: 1dc in each st to end. (24)

Rnd 34: [1dc, dc2tog] 8 times. (16)

Rnds 35-36: 1dc in each st to end. (16)

With flesh yarn

Rnd 37: dc2tog 8 times. (8)

Rnd 38: [2dc in next st, 1dc] 4 times. (12)

Rnd 39: 2dc in next st to end. (24)

Rnds 40-43: 1dc in each st to end. (24)

Rnd 44: 1dc in each st, until you get to the middle of the face, 4htrcl in next st, 1dc in each st to end. (24)

Rnds 45-47: 1dc in each st to end. (24)

Sew on beard and attach eyes.

Rnd 48: [dc2tog, 2dc] 6 times. (18)

Rnd 49: [dc2tog, 1dc] 6 times. (12)

Rnd 50: dc2tog until hole closes.

SHIRT

With white yarn

Ch16

Row 1: 1dc in 2nd ch from hook, 1dc in each st to end, turn. (15)

Row 2: 1ch, 1dc in each st to end, turn. (15)

With silver yarn

Row 3: 1ch, 1dc in each st to end, turn. (15)

Row 4: 1ch, [2dc, 2dc in next st] 5 times, turn. (20)

Row 5: 1ch, 1dc in each st to end, turn. (20)

Row 6: 1ch, [3dc, 2dc in next st] 5 times, turn. (25)

Row 7: 1ch, 1dc in each st to end, turn. (25)

Row 8: 1ch, [4dc, 2dc in next st] 5 times, turn. (30)

Row 9: 1ch, 1dc in each st to end, turn. (30)

Row 10: 1ch, [2dc, 2dc in next st] 10 times, turn. (40)

Rows 11-19: 1ch, 1dc in each st to end, turn. (40)

Shirt instructions continue after the shirt border.

SHIRT BORDER

Left side

With burgundy yarn

Row 1: Work 1ch, 1dc in the side of each stitch across the sides of the top up to row 3 of the shirt.

Fasten off.

Row 2: Begin row 2 at the same end you began row 1, 1ch, 2dc, [*with black yarn,* 1dc, *with burgundy yarn* 2dc] to end.

Fasten off.

Row 3: Begin row 3 at the same end you began row 2. 1ch, 1dc in each st to end.

Repeat this on the right side of the shirt border, this time starting at the top, just below row 2 of the main shirt.

Shirt continued

With white yarn

Row 20: 1ch, 1dc in each st to end, turn. (46)

With light grey yarn

Row 21: *8ch, 1tr in 4th ch from the hook, 1tr, 2htr, 1dc, sl st in next st of row 20, sl st in next st, rep from * until end.

Wrap shirt around body, and sew.

COAT

With gold yarn

Ch31

Row 1: 1dc in 2nd ch from hook, 1dc in each st to end, turn. (30)

With burgundy yarn

Rows 2-27: 1ch, 1dc in each st to end, turn. (30)

With white chunky yarn, using larger hook 1ch, 1dc in each st across the side of the jacket, 2dc in the corner st, 1dc across the bottom, 2dc in the corner st, 1dc up the other side of the jacket.

'We all are men, in our own nature's frail, and capable of our flesh; few are angels.'

Henry VIII (Act V, Scene 3)

ARMS

(Make 2)

With flesh yarn

Rnd 1: 8dc in magic ring. (8)

Rnds 2-4: 1dc in each st to end. (8)

With grey yarn

Rnd 5 *in blo*: 1dc in each st to end. (8)

Rnds 6-14: 1dc in each st to end. (8)

With white yarn

Into front loops of rnd 4, 2ch, 2htr in next st, [1htr, 2htr in next st] 3 times. (12)

Wrap coat around body and sew arms onto sides of body.

CHAIN

With gold yarn

Row 1: 4ch, 1dc in 2ch from hook, 2dc. (3)

Rows 2-40 *in blo*: 1ch, 1dc in each st to end. (3)

Use scraps of different colours to embroider on the jewels.

Sew one end to the side of the other one.

HAT

With black yarn

Rnd 1: 8dc in magic ring. (8)

Rnd 2: 2dc in each st to end. (16)

Rnd 3: [2dc in next st, 1dc] 8 times. (24)

Rnd 4: [2dc in next st, 2dc] 8 times. (32)

Rnd 5: [2dc in next st, 3dc] 8 times. (40)

Rnds 6-9: 1dc in each st to end. (40)

Rnd 10: 3ch, 2tr in next st, [1tr, 2tr in next st] 19 times. (60)

With white faux fur yarn, using larger hook

Rnd 11: 1ch, 1dc in each st to end, sl st to neaten. (60)

Make hair cap (see page 125) with orange yarn and sew onto head.

Cardinal Wolsey

YARN

100% cotton 4ply in white, flesh, black, red

SUGGESTED YARN:
'Must-have' from Yarn and Colors: White, Peach, Black, Cardinal

OTHER MATERIALS

2.5 mm (C/2) crochet hook
Yarn needle
6 mm (1/3 in) safety eyes x 2
Stitch marker
Fibrefill stuffing

PATTERN NOTES

- For htrcl stitch instructions, see page 124.
- Black yarn is notoriously hard to crochet with. As most of Wolsey's body will be hidden under his robe, you may wish to use another colour from round 8 of the legs.

ROBE

With red yarn
Ch16, join with sl st
Rnd 1: 1dc in each st to end, join. (16)
Rnd 2: [3dc, 2dc in next st] 4 times, join. (20)
Rnds 3-4: 1dc in next st to end, join. (20)
Rnd 5: [3dc, 2dc in next st] 5 times, join. (25)
Rnd 6: 1dc in each st to end, join. (25)
Rnd 7: [4dc, 2dc in next st] 5 times, join. (30)
Rnds 8-13: 1dc in each st to end, join. (30)
Rnd 14: [5dc, 2dc in next st] 5 times, join. (35)
Rnds 15-32: 1dc in each st to end, join. (35)

COLLAR

With red yarn
Ch24, sl st to join
Rnd 1: 1dc in each ch to end, join. (24)
Rnd 2: 1ch, [2dc, 2dc in next st] 8 times, join. (32)
Rnd 3: 1ch, 1dc in each st to end, join. (32)
Rnd 4: 1ch, [3dc, 2dc in next st] 8 times, join. (40)
Rnds 5-7: 1ch, 1dc in each st to end, join. (40)

RIGHT LEG

With black yarn
Rnd 1: 6ch, 1dc in 2nd ch from hook, 3dc, 4dc in next st, work remaining sts along the other side of the chs, 3dc, 3dc in next st, join. (14)
Work in spirals in continuous rounds without joining (unless otherwise stated), moving stitch marker up each round.
Rnd 2: 3dc, [2dc in next st] 4 times, 3dc, [2dc in next st] 4 times. (22)
Rnd 3 *in blo*: 3dc, [dc2tog] 4 times, 3dc, [dc2tog] 4 times. (14)
Rnd 4: 2dc, [dc2tog] 4 times, 1dc in each st to end. (10)
Rnd 5: 2dc, [dc2tog] twice, 1dc in each st to end. (8)
Rnds 6-13: 1dc in each st to end. (8)

LEFT LEG, BODY AND HEAD

With black yarn
Rnd 1: 6ch, 1dc in 2nd ch from hook, 3dc, 4dc in next st, work remaining sts along the other side of the chs, 3dc, 3dc in next st, join. (14)
Work in spirals in continuous rounds without joining (unless otherwise stated), moving stitch marker up each round.
Rnd 2: 3dc, [2dc in next st] 4 times, 3dc, [2dc in next st] 4 times. (22)
Rnd 3 *in blo*: 3dc, [dc2tog] 4 times, 3dc, [dc2tog] 4 times. (14)
Rnd 4: 2dc, [dc2tog] 4 times, 1dc in each st to end. (10)
Rnd 5: 2dc, [dc2tog] twice, 1dc in each st to end. (8)
Rnds 6-13: 1dc in each st to end. (8)
The rest of the body will not be seen so you may wish to work in a lighter colour instead of black.

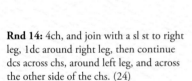

*'The king has gone beyond
me: all my glories
In that one woman
I have lost for ever:
No sun shall ever usher
forth mine honours,
Or gild again the noble
troops that waited
Upon my smiles.'*
(Act III, Scene 3)

Rnd 14: 4ch, and join with a sl st to right leg, 1dc around right leg, then continue dcs across chs, around left leg, and across the other side of the chs. (24)

Rnds 15-27: 1dc in each st to end. (24)

Rnd 28: [4dc, dc2tog] 4 times. (20)

Rnd 29: 1dc in each st to end. (20)

Rnd 30: [3dc, dc2tog] 4 times. (16)

Rnd 31: 1dc in each st to end. (16)

With flesh yarn

Rnd 32: [2dc, dc2tog] 4 times. (12)

Rnd 33: [1dc, dc2tog] 4 times. (8)

Rnd 34: 1dc in each st to end. (8)

Rnd 35: [2dc in st, 1dc] 4 times. (12)

Rnd 36: 2dc in each st to end. (24)

Add the robe and collar.

Rnds 37-40: 1dc in each st to end. (24)

Rnd 41: 1dc in each st until you get to the middle of the face, 4htrcl in next st, 1dc in each st to end. (24)

Rnds 42-44: 1dc in each st to end. (24)

Rnd 45: [dc2tog, 2dc] 6 times. (18)

Rnd 46: [dc2tog, 1dc] 6 times. (12)

Rnd 47: dc2tog until hole closes.

ARMS

(Make 2)

With flesh yarn

Rnd 1: 8dc in magic ring. (8)

Rnds 2-4: 1dc in each st to end. (8)

With black yarn

Rnds 5-14: 1dc in each st to end. (8)

Sew onto sides of body.

Make hair cap in grey, (see page 125) and sew onto head.

HAT

With red yarn

Rnd 1: 6dc in magic ring. (6)

Rnd 2: 2dc in each st to end. (12)

Rnd 3: [2dc in next st, 1dc] 6 times. (18)

Rnd 4: [2dc in next st, 2dc] 6 times. (24)

Rnd 5 *in blo*: 1dc in each st to end. (24)

Rnds 6-8: 1dc in each st to end. (24)

YARN

100% cotton 4ply in light green, flesh, dark green, brown, white

SUGGESTED YARN:
'Must-have' from Yarn and Colors: Peony Leaf, Peach, Forest, Brunet, White

OTHER MATERIALS

2.5 mm (C/2) crochet hook
Yarn needle
6 mm (1/3 in) safety eyes x 2
Stitch marker
Fibrefill stuffing

PATTERN NOTES

- For htrcl stitch instructions, see page 124.
- For hair instructions, see page 125.

Anne Boleyn

RIGHT LEG

With green yarn
Rnd 1: 6ch, 1dc in 2nd ch from hook, 3dc, 4dc in next st, work remaining sts along the other side of the chs, 3dc, 3dc in next st, join. (14)
Work in spirals in continuous rounds without joining (unless otherwise stated), moving stitch marker up each round.
Rnd 2: 3dc, [2dc in next st] 4 times, 3dc, [2dc in next st] 4 times. (22)
Rnd 3 in blo: 3dc, [dc2tog] 4 times, 3dc, [dc2tog] 4 times. (14)
Rnd 4: 2dc, [dc2tog] 4 times, 1dc in each st to end. (10)
With flesh yarn
Rnd 5: 2dc, [dc2tog] twice, 1dc in each st to end. (8)
Rnds 6-13: 1dc in each st to end. (8)

LEFT LEG, BODY AND HEAD

With green yarn
Rnd 1: 6ch, 1dc in 2nd ch from hook, 3dc, 4dc in next st, work remaining sts along the other side of the chs, 3dc, 3dc in next st, join. (14)
Work in spirals in continuous rounds without joining (unless otherwise stated), moving stitch marker up each round.
Rnd 2: 3dc, [2dc in next st] 4 times, 3dc, [2dc in next st] 4 times. (22)
Rnd 3 in blo: 3dc, [dc2tog] 4 times, 3dc, [dc2tog] 4 times. (14)
Rnd 4: 2dc, [dc2tog] 4 times, 1dc in each st to end. (10)
With flesh yarn
Rnd 5: 2dc, [dc2tog] twice, 1dc in each st to end. (8)
Rnds 6-13: 1dc in each st to end. (8)
With green yarn
Rnd 14: 4ch, join with a sl st to right leg, 1dc in each st around right leg, then

continue 1dc in each st across chs, around left leg and across the other side of the chs. (24)

Rnds 15-19: 1dc in each st to end. (24)

Rnds 20-21 *in blo:* 1dc in each st to end. (24)

Rnds 22-27: 1dc in each st to end. (24)

Rnd 28: [4dc, dc2tog] 4 times. (20)

Rnd 29: 1dc in each st to end. (20)

With gold yarn

NB: Be aware of where the end of your round is as the colour changes might be too obvious if its at the front. You may prefer to finish with a colour mid-way through a round at the back, so Anne looks a bit neater.

Rnd 30: [3dc, dc2tog] 4 times. (16)

With flesh yarn

Rnd 31: 1dc in each st to end. (16)

Rnd 32: [2dc, dc2tog] 4 times. (12)

Rnd 33: [1dc, dc2tog] 4 times. (8)

Rnd 34: 1dc in each st to end. (8)

Rnd 35: [2dc in next st, 1dc] 4 times. (12)

Rnd 36: 2dc in each st to end. (24)

Rnds 37-40: 1dc in each st to end. (24)

Rnd 41: 1dc in each st, until you get to the middle of the face, 4htrcl in next st, 1dc in each st to end. (24)

Rnds 42-44: 1dc in each st to end. (24)

Add eyes, sew on a mouth.

Rnd 45: [dc2tog, 2dc] 6 times. (18)

Rnd 46: [dc2tog, 1dc] 6 times. (12)

Rnd 47: dc2tog until hole closes.

UNDERSKIRT

With dark green yarn

Turn Anne upside down and work into the front loops of round 20, join the at the back.

Rnd 1: 2ch, [2htr in next st, 1htr] 11 times, 2htr in next st, join with a sl st. (36)

Rnds 2-9: 2ch, 1htr in each st to end. (36)

With green yarn

Rnd 10: 1ch, 1dc in each st to end. (36)

OUTERSKIRT

With green yarn

Keeping Anne turned upside down, work into the front loops of round 21, start from 2sts to the left of the middle.

Row 1: 1ch, 1dc, [2dc in next st] 20 times, 1dc, leave the remaining 2sts in the middle unworked, turn. (42)

Rows 2-19: 1ch, 1dc in each st to end, turn. (42)

With gold yarn

Begin at the top of ones of the sides, 1dc along the side of the row until you get to the corner, 3dc in corner, 1dc in each st along the bottom until the corner, 3dc in corner, 1dc in each st until you're back at the top of outerskirt, join to the first gold stitch.

ARMS

(Make 2)

With flesh yarn

Rnd 1: 8dc in magic ring. (8)

Rnds 2-4: 1dc in each st to end. (8)

With green yarn

Rnds 5-14: 1dc in each st to end. (8)

Sew to sides of body.

Make hair with brown yarn (see page 125), sew onto head.

HEADDRESS

With dark green yarn

Ch3

Row 1: 9htr in first ch, turn. (10)

Row 2: 2ch, [2htr in next st] 8 times, 1htr, turn. (18)

Row 3: 2ch, [2htr in next st, 1htr] 7 times, 1htr, turn. (25)

Row 4: 2ch, 1htr in each st to end, turn. (25)

With green yarn

Row 5: 1ch, 1dc in each st to end. (25)

'I swear,' 'tis better to be lowly born,
And range with humble livers in content,
Than to be perk'd up in a glistering grief,
And wear a golden sorrow.'

Anne (Act II, Scene 3)

Julius Caesar

'The fault, dear Brutus, is not in our stars,
But in ourselves.'

Julius Caesar (Act I, Scene 2)

Julius Caesar returns to Rome, triumphant from a war against Pompey, and is lauded and honoured by the Republic. The celebrations cause concern among members of the Senate that just one man has too much power and that he could seek to become Emperor. Caesar is warned by a soothsayer to 'Beware the Ides [15th] of March.' An assassination plot unfolds, and Brutus is eventually persuaded to take part in the conspiracy. On the Ides of March, Caesar is stabbed by his senators, including the final blow from his friend, Brutus.

Shakespeare looked to ancient Rome as inspiration for many of his works, including *Titus Andronicus*, *Coriolanus* and *Antony and Cleopatra*. His source for this play was the work of first-century historian Plutarch, and the events which took place in 44 BC. *Julius Caesar* was probably one of the first plays performed at the Globe Theatre in the late 1500s in London.

YARN

100% cotton 4ply in brown, flesh, white, purple, gold, green, grey

SUGGESTED YARN:
'Must-have' from Yarn and Colors: Brownie, Peach, White, Lilac, Mustard, Grass, Shark Grey

OTHER MATERIALS

2.5 mm (C/2) crochet hook
Yarn needle
6 mm (1/3 in) safety eyes x 2
Stitch marker
Fibrefill stuffing

PATTERN NOTES

- For htrcl stitch instructions, see page 124.
- For hair instructions, see page 125.
- The chart shows a section of the beginning and end of the crown.
- For further details of how to read charts see page 127.

Julius Caesar

TUNIC

With yellow yarn
Ch18, join with sl st
Rnd 1: 1ch, [1dc, 2dc in next st] 9 times, join. (27)
With purple yarn
Rnd 2: 1ch, 1dc in each st to end, join. (27)
With white yarn
Rnds 3-14: 2ch, 1htr in each st to end, join. (27)
With purple yarn
Rnd 15: 1ch, 1dc in each st to end, join. (27)
With yellow yarn
Rnd 16: 1ch, 1dc in each st to end, join. (27)

RIGHT LEG

With brown yarn
Rnd 1: 6ch, 1dc in 2nd ch from hook, 3dc, 4dc in next st, work remaining sts along the other side of the chs, 3dc, 3dc in next st, join. (14)
Work in spirals in continuous rounds without joining (unless otherwise stated), moving stitch marker up each round.
Rnd 2: 3dc, [2dc in next st] 4 times, 3dc,

[2dc in next st] 4 times. (22)
With flesh yarn
Rnd 3 in blo: 3dc, [dc2tog] 4 times, 3dc, [dc2tog] 4 times. (14)
Rnd 4: 2dc, [dc2tog] 4 times, 1dc in each st to end. (10)
Rnd 5: 2dc, [dc2tog] twice, 1dc in each st to end. (8)
Rnds 6-13: 1dc in each st to end. (8)

LEFT LEG, BODY AND HEAD

With brown yarn
Rnd 1: 6ch, 1dc in 2nd ch from hook, 3dc, 4dc in next st, work remaining sts along the other side of the chs, 3dc, 3dc in next st, join. (14)
Work in spirals in continuous rounds without joining (unless otherwise stated), moving stitch marker up each round.
Rnd 2: 3dc, [2dc in next st] 4 times, 3dc, [2dc in next st] 4 times. (22)
With flesh yarn
Rnd 3 in blo: 3dc, [dc2tog] 4 times, 3dc, [dc2tog] 4 times. (14)
Rnd 4: 2dc, [dc2tog] 4 times, 1dc in each st to end. (10)
Rnd 5: 2dc, [dc2tog] twice, 1dc in each st to end. (8)
Rnds 6-13: 1dc in each st to end. (8)

Rnd 14: 4ch, and join with a sl st to right leg, 1dc around right leg, then continue dcs across chs, around left leg, and across the other side of the chs. (24)

Rnds 15-27: 1dc in each st to end. (24)

Rnd 28: [4dc, dc2tog] 4 times. (20)

Rnd 29: 1dc in each st to end. (20)

Rnd 30: [3dc, dc2tog] 4 times. (16)

Rnd 31: 1dc in each st to end. (16)

Rnd 32: [2dc, dc2tog] 4 times. (12)

Rnd 33: [1dc, dc2tog] 4 times. (8)

Rnd 34: 1dc in each st to end. (8)

Rnd 35: [2dc in next st, 1dc] 4 times. (12)

Place tunic over the neck - you may need to snip the yarn and then reattach it.

Rnd 36: 2dc in each st to end. (24)

Rnds 37-40: 1dc in each st to end. (24)

Rnd 41: 1dc in each st, until you get to the middle of the face, 4htrcl in next st, 1dc in each st to end. (24)

Rnds 42-44: 1dc in each st to end. (24)

Attach eyes, and sew on mouth.

Rnd 45: [dc2tog, 2dc] 6 times. (18)

Rnd 46: [dc2tog, 1dc] 6 times. (12)

Rnd 47: dc2tog until hole closes.

ARMS

With flesh yarn

Rnd 1: 8dc in magic ring. (8)

Rnds 2-14: 1dc in each st to end. (8)

Sew onto sides of body.

SLEEVES

With white yarn

Ch4

Row 1: 9tr in first ch, turn. (10)

Row 2: 3ch, 1tr in next st as starting chs, 8tr, 2tr in last st, turn. (12)

With purple yarn

Row 3: 1ch, 1dc in each st to end, turn. (12)

With gold yarn

Row 4: 1ch, 1dc in each st to end. (12)

Sew onto arms and body.

TOGA

With purple yarn

Ch6

Row 1: 1dc in 2nd ch from hook, 1dc in each st to end, turn. (5)

Rows 2-112: 1ch, 1dc in each st to end, turn. (5)

BORDER

With yellow yarn

Working around the entire piece, join just after a corner, 1ch, 1dc in each st, until you get to corner, 3dc in corner, continue with 1dc in each st around the purple.

Make hair in grey (see page 125), sew onto head.

LAUREL CROWN

With green yarn

Ch40

Sl st in 2nd ch from hook, 1htr in next st, sl st, *[3ch, sl st into 2nd ch from hook, 1dc in next ch, sl st into main chain where this stitch started from, 3sl st] repeat from until the end of the chain, then work around the other side, into the bottom of the sts.

Sew onto hair.

SHOES

With brown yarn

Ch20

Fold, sew a few stitches together in the middle, and sew onto feet.

'Et tu, Brute?
Then fall, Caesar.'

Julius Caesar
(Act III, Scene 1)

LAUREL CROWN CHART

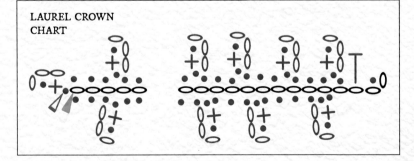

YARN

100% cotton 4ply in brown, flesh, white, red

SUGGESTED YARN:

'Must-have' from Yarn and Colors:
Brownie, Rosé, White, Burgundy

OTHER MATERIALS

2.5 mm (C/2) crochet hook
Yarn needle
6 mm (1/3 in) safety eyes x 2
Stitch marker
Fibrefill stuffing

PATTERN NOTES

- For htrcl stitch instructions,
  see page 124.
- For hair instructions,
  see page 125.

Brutus

TUNIC

With white yarn
Ch18, join with sl st
Rnd 1: 2ch, [2htr in next st, 1htr] 9 times,
join. (28)
Rnds 2-15: 2ch, 1htr in each st to end,
join. (28)
With burgundy yarn
Rnd 16: 1ch, 1dc in each st to end, join.
(28)

RIGHT LEG

With brown yarn
Rnd 1: 6ch, 1dc in 2nd ch from hook,
3dc, 4dc in next st, work remaining sts
along the other side of the chs, 3dc, 3dc in
next st, join. (14)
*Work in spirals in continuous rounds without
joining (unless otherwise stated), moving
stitch marker up each round.*
Rnd 2: 3dc, [2dc in next st] 4 times, 3dc,
[2dc in next st] 4 times. (22)
With flesh yarn

Rnd 3 *in blo:* 3dc, [dc2tog] 4 times, 3dc,
[dc2tog] 4 times. (14)
Rnd 4: 2dc, [dc2tog] 4 times, 1dc in each
st to end. (10)
Rnd 5: 2dc, [dc2tog] twice, 1dc in each st
to end. (8)
Rnds 6-13: 1dc in each st to end. (8)

LEFT LEG AND BODY

With brown yarn
Rnd 1: 6ch, 1dc in 2nd ch from hook,
3dc, 4dc in next st, work remaining sts
along the other side of the chs, 3dc, 3dc in
next st, join. (14)
*For the remaining rounds do not join unless
otherwise stated. Place a stitch marker in the
first stitch of a round.*
Rnd 2: 3dc, [2dc in next st] 4 times, 3dc,
[2dc in next st] 4 times. (22)
With flesh yarn
Rnd 3 *in blo:* 3dc, [dc2tog] 4 times, 3dc,
[dc2tog] 4 times. (14)
Rnd 4: 2dc, [dc2tog] 4 times, 1dc in each
st to end. (10)
Rnd 5: 2dc, [dc2tog] twice, 1dc in each st
to end. (8)
Rnds 6-13: 1dc in each st to end. (8)
With white yarn
Rnd 14: 4ch, and join with a sl st to right

leg, 1dc around right leg, then continue dcs across chs, around left leg, and across the other side of the chs. (24)

Rnds 15-19: 1dc in each st to end. (24)

With flesh yarn

Rnds 20-27: 1dc in each st to end. (24)

Rnd 28: [4dc, dc2tog] 4 times. (20)

Rnd 29: 1dc in each st to end. (20)

Rnd 30: [3dc, dc2tog] 4 times. (16)

Rnd 31: 1dc in each st to end. (16)

Rnd 32: [2dc, dc2tog] 4 times. (12)

Rnd 33: [1dc, dc2tog] 4 times. (8)

Rnd 34: 1dc in each st to end. (8)

Rnd 35: [2dc in next st, 1dc] 4 times. (12)

Place tunic over the neck - you may need to cut the yarn and then reattach it.

Rnd 36: 2dc in each st to end. (24)

Rnds 37-40: 1dc in each st to end. (24)

Rnd 41: 1dc in each st until you get to the middle of the face, 4htrcl in next st, 1dc in each st to end. (24)

Rnds 42-44: 1dc in each st to end. (24)

Attach eyes and sew on mouth.

Rnd 45: [dc2tog, 2dc] 6 times. (18)

Rnd 46: [dc2tog, 1dc] 6 times. (12)

Rnd 47: dc2tog until hole closes.

ARMS

(Make 2)

With flesh yarn

Rnd 1: 8dc in magic ring. (8)

Rnds 2-14: 1dc in each st. (8)

SLEEVES

(Make 2)

With white yarn

Ch3

Row 1: 5tr in 3rd ch from hook, turn. (6)

Row 2: 2ch, 1htr in next st, 4htr, 2htr in last st, turn. (8)

Row 3: 2ch, 1htr in next st, 6htr, 2htr in last st, turn. (10)

With burgundy yarn

Row 4: 1ch, 1dc in each st to end. (10)

TOGA

With white yarn

Ch7

Row 1: 1dc in 2nd ch from hook, 1dc in each st to end, turn. (6)

Rows 2-112: 1ch, 1dc in each st to end, turn. (6)

With burgundy yarn

Along one of the lengths only, 1ch, 1dc in each st across the entire length.

Make hair in brown, see page 125 for instructions.

SHOES

(Make 2)

With brown yarn

Ch7

Sew to sides of foot to create a sandal look.

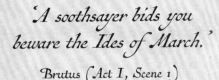

'A soothsayer bids you beware the Ides of March.'

Brutus (Act I, Scene 1)

King Lear

'When we are born, we cry that we are
come to this great stage of fools.'

King Lear (Act IV, Scene 5)

Ageing King Lear is ready to retire and divide up his kingdom so asks
his three daughters how much they love him. The older two, Goneril
and Regan, satisfy him with platitudes but the younger, Cordelia,
can't express her love in words – which angers Lear and he disowns
her, splitting his realm between the other two. Lear and 100 knights
stay with both Goneril and Regan who grow frustrated hosting the
entourage. Lear is angered by their disrespect and departs with his fool
at his side into the stormy night. Lear loses his mind and upon hearing
this, Cordelia reunites with him and battle ensues against her sisters.

It is thought Shakespeare wrote *King Lear* while plague raged in
London and theatres were forced to shut. He based it on the legend
of a King Lier – who may have founded the city of Leicester and
ruled around 8th Century BC. The fool as the actual wise man of the
play was also used in *Twelfth Night* and *As You Like It*. *King Lear* was
immensely popular but performances of the play were banned for ten
years during the reign of King George III, who towards the end of
his 60-year reign displayed erratic behaviour, which may have
been caused by mental illness and blood disorder.

YARN

100% cotton 4ply in grey, flesh, white, purple, gold, royal blue

SUGGESTED YARN:
'Must-have' from Yarn and Colors: Shark Grey, Peach, Lilac, Mustard, Sapphire

OTHER MATERIALS

2.5 mm (C/2) crochet hook
Yarn needle
6 mm (1/3 in) safety eyes x 2
Stitch marker
Fibrefill stuffing

PATTERN NOTES

- For htrcl stitch instructions, see page 124.
- For further details of how to read charts see page 127.

King Lear

TUNIC

With gold yarn
Ch18, join with a sl st.
Rnd 1: 1ch, [1dc, 2dc in next st] 9 times, join. (27)
With purple
Rnd 2: 2ch, 2htr in next st, 1htr in each st to end, join. (28)
Rnds 3-8: 2ch, 1htr in each st to end, join. (28)
Rnd 9: 2ch, 2htr, [2htr in next st, 3htr] 6 times, 2htr in last st. (35)
Rnds 10-16: 2ch, 1htr in each st to end. (35)
With gold yarn
Rnd 17: 1ch, 1dc in each st to end. (35)

HAIR

With white yarn
Ch16
Row 1: 1htr in 3rd ch from hook, 1htr in each st to end, turn. (14)
Row 2: 2ch, [2htr in next st, 1htr] 7 times, turn. (21)
Rows 3-4: 2ch, 1htr in each st to end, turn. (21)

BEARD

With white yarn
Ch16
Row 1: 1dc in 2nd ch from hook, 1dc to end, turn. (15)
Row 2: 1ch, 5dc, 5ch, miss 5 chs, 5dc, turn. (15)
Rows 3-4: 1ch, 1dc in each st to end, turn. (15)

RIGHT LEG

With grey yarn
Rnd 1: 6ch, 1dc in 2nd ch from hook, 3dc, 4dc in next st, work remaining sts along the other side of the chs, 3dc, 3dc in next st, join. (14)
Work in spirals in continuous rounds without joining (unless otherwise stated), moving stitch marker up each round.
Rnd 2: 3dc, [2dc in next st] 4 times, 3dc, [2dc in next st] 4 times. (22)
Rnd 3 in blo: 3dc, [dc2tog] 4 times, 3dc, [dc2tog] 4 times. (14)
Rnd 4: 2dc, [dc2tog] 4 times, 1dc in each st to end. (10)
Rnd 5: 2dc, [dc2tog] twice, 1dc in each st to end. (8)
With flesh yarn
Rnds 6-13: 1dc in each st to end. (8)

LEFT LEG AND BODY

With grey yarn

Rnd 1: 6ch, 1dc in 2nd ch from hook, 3dc, 4dc in next st, work remaining sts along the other side of the chs, 3dc, 3dc in next st, join. (14)

Work in spirals in continuous rounds without joining (unless otherwise stated), moving stitch marker up each round.

Rnd 2: 3dc, [2dc in next st] 4 times, 3dc, [2dc in next st] 4 times. (22)

Rnd 3 in blo: 3dc, [dc2tog] 4 times, 3dc, [dc2tog] 4 times. (14)

Rnd 4: 2dc, [dc2tog] 4 times, 1dc in each st to end. (10)

Rnd 5: 2dc, [dc2tog] twice, 1dc in each st to end. (8)

With flesh yarn

Rnds 6-13: 1dc in each st to end. (8)

With white yarn

Rnd 14: 4ch, and join with a sl st to right leg, 1dc around right leg, then continue dcs across chs, around left leg, and across the other side of the chs. (24)

Rnds 15-27: 1dc in each st to end. (24)

Rnd 28: [4dc, dc2tog] 4 times. (20)

Rnd 29: 1dc in each st to end. (20)

Rnd 30: [3dc, dc2tog] 4 times. (16)

Rnd 31: 1dc in each st to end. (16)

With flesh yarn

Rnd 32: [2dc, dc2tog] 4 times. (12)

Rnd 33: [1dc, dc2tog] 4 times. (8)

Rnd 34: 1dc in each st to end. (8)

Add tunic.

Rnd 35: [2dc in next st, 1dc] 4 times. (12)

Rnd 36: 2dc in each st to end. (24)

Rnds 37-40: 1dc in each st to end. (24)

Rnd 41: 1dc in each st until you get to the middle of the face, 4htrcl in next st, 1dc in each st to end. (24)

Rnds 42-44: 1dc in each st to end. (24)

Attach eyes, sew on beard and hair.

Rnd 45: [dc2tog, 2dc] 6 times. (18)

Rnd 46: [dc2tog, 1dc] 6 times. (12)

Rnd 47: dc2tog until hole closes.

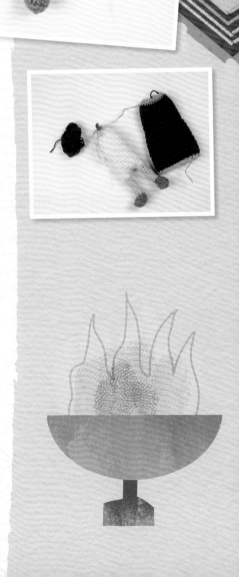

CAPE

With royal blue yarn

Ch13

Row 1: 1htr in 3rd ch from hook, 1htr in each st to end, turn. (12)

Row 2: 2ch, [2htr in next st, 1htr] 5 times, 2htr in last st, turn. (18)

Row 3: 2ch, [2htr in next st, 2htr] 5 times, 2htr in next st, 1htr, turn. (24)

Rows 4-16: 2ch, 1htr in each st to end, turn. (24)

BORDER

With gold yarn

Begin at the side of row 1, 1ch, work dcs into the sides of the stitches down to the corner, 3dcs into the corner, 1dc in each st along row 16, 3dcs into the corner, work dcs into the sides of the stitches up to the other end of row 1, 20ch.

'Blow winds and crack your cheeks!
Rage, blow, you cataracts and hurricanoes.'

Lear (Act III, Scene 2)

CROWN CHART

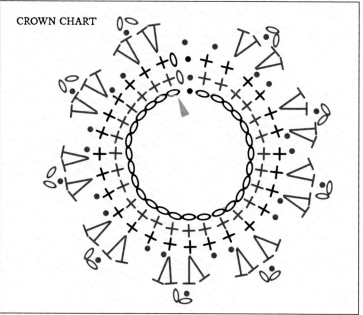

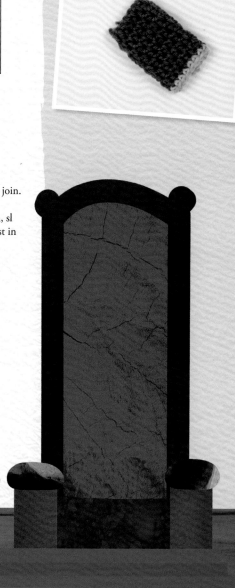

SLEEVES

(Make 2)

With purple yarn

Ch15, sl st to join.

Rnds 1-7: 2ch, 1htr in each st to end, join. (15)

With gold yarn

Rnd 8: 1ch, 1dc in each st to end. (15)

ARMS

(Make 2)

With flesh yarn

Rnd 1: 8dc in magic ring. (8)

Rnds 2-14: 1dc in each st to end. (8)

Attach arms to the side of the tunic.

Sew sleeves on to the tunic.

CROWN

With yellow yarn

Ch27, sl st to join.

Rnds 1-2: 1ch, 1dc in each st to end, join. (27)

Rnd 3: [miss 1 st, 2htr in next st, 2ch, sl st in 2nd ch from hook, 2htr in next st in rnd 2, sl st in next 2 sts] 6 times.

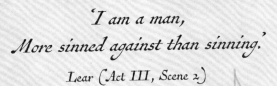

'I am a man,
More sinned against than sinning.'

Lear (Act III, Scene 2)

Lear's Fool

TUNIC

With green yarn
Ch18, join with sl st
Rnd 1: 2ch, 1htr, [2htr in next st, 2htr] 5 times, 2htr in next st, join. (24)
Rnd 2: 2ch, 2htr, 2htr in next st, [3htr, 2htr in next st] 5 times, join. (30)
Rnds 3-10: 2ch, 1htr in each st to end, join. (30)
Rnd 11: [4ch, sl st in first ch from hook, 1dc in next ch, 1htr in last ch, miss 1 st in rnd 10, sl st in next st of rnd 10, sl st in to next st] 10 times.

COLLAR

With purple yarn
Ch21, join with sl st.
Rnd 1: [4ch, sl st in first ch from hook, 1dc in next ch, 1htr in last ch, miss 1 st in ch ring, sl st in next st of chs, sl st in to next st] 7 times.
Sew onto tunic.

RIGHT LEG

With purple yarn
Rnd 1: 6ch, 1dc in 2nd ch from hook, 3dc, 4dc in next st, work remaining sts along the other side of the chs, 3dc, 3dc in next st, join. (14)
Work in spirals in continuous rounds without joining (unless otherwise stated), moving stitch marker up each round.
Rnd 2: 3dc, [2dc in next st] 4 times, 3dc, [2dc in next st] 4 times. (22)
Rnd 3: 3dc, [dc2tog] 4 times, 3dc, [dc2tog] 4 times. (14)
Rnd 4: 2dc, [dc2tog] 4 times, 1dc in each st to end. (10)
Rnd 5: 2dc, [dc2tog] twice, 1dc in each st to end. (8)
Rnd 6 *in blo:* 1dc in each st to end. (8)
With blue yarn
Rnds 7-13: 1dc in each st to end. (8)

LEFT LEG, BODY AND HEAD

With purple yarn
Rnd 1: 6ch, 1dc in 2nd ch from hook, 3dc, 4dc in next st, work remaining sts along the other side of the chs, 3dc, 3dc in next st, join. (14)
Work in spirals in continuous rounds without joining (unless otherwise stated), moving stitch marker up each round.

Rnd 2: 3dc, [2dc in next st] 4 times, 3dc, [2dc in next st] 4 times. (22)

Rnd 3: 3dc, [dc2tog] 4 times, 3dc, [dc2tog] 4 times. (14)

Rnd 4: 2dc, [dc2tog] 4 times, 1dc in each st to end. (10)

Rnd 5: 2dc, [dc2tog], 1dc in each st to end. (8)

Rnd 6 *in blo*: 1dc in each st to end. (8)
With blue yarn

Rnds 7-13: 1dc in each st to end. (8)

Rnd 14: 4ch, and join with a sl st to right leg, 1dc around right leg, then continue dcs across chs, around left leg, and across the other side of the chs. (24)
With white yarn

Rnds 15-27: 1dc in each st to end. (24)

Rnd 28: [4dc, dc2tog] 4 times. (20)

Rnd 29: 1dc in each st to end. (20)

Rnd 30: [3dc, dc2tog] 4 times. (16)

Rnd 31: 1dc in each st to end. (16)

Rnd 32: [2dc, dc2tog] 4 times. (12)

Rnd 33: [1dc, dc2tog] 4 times. (8)
Add tunic and collar.

Rnd 34: 1dc in each st to end. (8)

Rnd 35: [2dc in next st, 1dc] 4 times. (12)

Rnd 36: 2dc in each st to end. (24)

Rnds 37-40: 1dc in each st to end. (24)

Rnd 41: 1dc in each st, until you get to the middle of the face, 4htrcl in next st, 1dc to end. (24)

Rnds 42-44: 1dc in each st to end. (24)
Attach eyes and sew on a mouth.

Rnd 45: [dc2tog, 2dc] 6 times. (18)

Rnd 46: [dc2tog, 1dc] 6 times. (12)

Rnd 47: dc2tog until hole closes.

ARMS
(Make 2)
With flesh yarn

Rnd 1: 8dc in magic ring. (8)

Rnds 2-4: 1dc in each st to end. (8)
With red yarn

Rnds 5-14: 1dc in each st to end. (8)
Attach arms to body.

CUFFS
(Make 2)
With purple yarn
Ch15, join with a sl st.

Rnd 1: [3ch, sl st in 2nd ch from hook, 1htr in next ch, miss 1 st in loop, sl st in next st, sl st in next st] 6 times.
Attach to arms.

HAT
Bells
(Make 3)
With yellow yarn

Rnd 1: 6dc in magic ring. (6)

Rnd 2: 1dc in each st to end. (6)

Rnd 3: [dc2tog] 3 times. (3)
Use a needle to close the hole.

Piece 1
With green yarn

Rnd 1: 6dc in magic ring. (6)

Rnd 2: 2dc in each st to end. (12)

Rnd 3: [2dc in next st, 1dc] 6 times. (18)

Rnd 4: [2dc in next st, 2dc] 6 times. (24)

Rnd 5: [2dc in next st, 3dc] 6 times. (32)

Rnds 6-10: 1dc in each st to end. (32)

Piece 2
(Make 3)
One with purple yarn, one with red yarn and one with blue yarn

Rnd 1: 6dc in magic ring. (6)

Rnds 2-3: 1dc in each st to end. (6)
Sew bell on

Rnd 4: [1dc, 2dc in next st] 3 times. (9)

Rnd 5: 1dc in each st to end. (9)

Rnd 6: [1dc, 2dc in next st] 4 times, 1dc. (13)

Rnds 7-12: 1dc in each st to end. (13)
Stuff and attach to piece 1.

'Thou shouldst not have been old
till thou hadst been wise.'

Fool (Act I, Scene 5)

Much Ado About Nothing

*'But then there was a star danced
and under that I was born.'*

Beatrice (Act II, Scene 2)

After the war, the Prince Don Pedro and his entourage, including his illegitmate brother Don John, Benedick and Claudio arrive at house of Leonate – the Duke of Messina. The Duke's daughter Hero and niece Beatrice live there too and Claudio and Hero fall in love and get engaged. In contrast, Beatrice and Benedick, who despise the idea of love, engage in a merry war throwing insults at each other constantly. The friends decide to trick them into falling for each other, while Don John decides to ruin Claudio and Hero's wedding by casting doubts on her honour. Hero is jilted and fakes her own death but in the end love wins and both couples marry and everyone (except for the arrested Don John) parties.

Much Ado About Nothing is Shakespeare's most frequently performed comedy, featuring the warring pair who end up falling in love, and is worth watching just for the insults. This combative courtship has been used in literature throughout the ages and still endures in many of our modern-day romantic comedies. In the 16th century the writer Philip Sidney portrayed Cupid as a 'murdering boy' armed with a 'bloody bullet', rather than the cherub we see him as now,. The love-hate pairing of Beatrice and Benedick has been taken on by many famous actors over the years on stage and screen, Peggy Ashcroft and John Gielgud (1950), Judi Dench and Donald Sinden (1976), Emma Thompson and Kenneth Branagh (1993) and Vanessa Redgrave and James Earl Jones (2013) when they were in their 70s and 80s, respectively.

HERO

YARN

100% cotton 4ply in brown, grey, red, black, gold, white, flesh

SUGGESTED YARN:
'Must-have' from Yarn and Colors: Taupe, Shark Grey, Pepper, Black, Mustard, White, Peach

OTHER MATERIALS

2.5 mm (C/2) crochet hook
Yarn needle
6 mm (1/3 in) safety eyes x 2
Stitch marker
Fibrefill stuffing

PATTERN NOTES

- For htrcl stitch instructions, see page 124.
- For hair cap instructions, see page 125.

Benedick

RIGHT LEG

With brown yarn
Rnd 1: 6ch, 1dc in 2nd ch from hook, 3dc, 4dc in next st, work remaining sts along the other side of the chs, 3dc, 3dc in next st, join. (14)
Work in spirals in continuous rounds without joining (unless otherwise stated), moving stitch marker up each round.
Rnd 2: 3dc, [2dc in next st] 4 times, 3dc, [2dc in next st] 4 times. (22)
Rnd 3 *in blo*: 3dc, [dc2tog] 4 times, 3dc, [dc2tog] 4 times. (14)
Rnd 4: 2dc, [dc2tog] 4 times, 1dc in each st to end. (10)
Rnd 5: 2dc, [dc2tog] twice, 1dc in each st to end. (8)
Rnds 6-8: 1dc in each st to end. (8)
With grey yarn
Rnd 9 *in blo*: 1dc in each st to end. (8)
Rnds 10-13: 1dc in each st to end. (8)

LEFT LEG, BODY AND HEAD

With brown yarn
Rnd 1: 6ch, 1dc in 2nd ch from hook, 3dc, 4dc in next st, work remaining sts along the other side of the chs, 3dc, 3dc in next st, join. (14)
Work in spirals in continuous rounds without joining (unless otherwise stated), moving stitch marker up each round.
Rnd 2: 3dc, [2dc in next st] 4 times, 3dc, [2dc in next st] 4 times. (22)
Rnd 3 *in blo*: 3dc, [dc2tog] 4 times, 3dc, [dc2tog] 4 times. (14)
Rnd 4: 2dc, [dc2tog] 4 times, 1dc in each st to end. (10)

Rnd 5: 2dc, [dc2tog] twice, 1dc in each st to end. (8)

Rnds 6-8: 1dc in each st to end. (8)

With grey yarn

Rnd 9 *in blo*: 1dc in each st to end. (8)

Rnds 10-13: 1dc in each st to end. (8)

Rnd 14: 4ch, and join with a sl st to right leg, 1dc around right leg, then continue dcs across chs, around left leg, and across the other side of the chs. (24)

Rnds 15-27: 1dc in each st to end. (24)

Rnd 28: [4dc, dc2tog] 4 times. (20)

Rnd 29: 1dc in each st to end. (20)

Rnd 30: [3dc, dc2tog] 4 times. (16)

Rnd 31: 1dc in each st to end. (16)

With flesh yarn

Rnd 32: [2dc, dc2tog] 4 times. (12)

Rnd 33: [1dc, dc2tog] 4 times. (8)

Rnd 34: 1dc in each st to end. (8)

Rnd 35: [2dc in next st, 1dc] 4 times. (12)

Rnd 36: 2dc in each st to end. (24)

Rnds 37-40: 1dc in each st to end. (24)

Rnd 41: 1dc in each st until you get to the middle of the face, 4htrcl in next st, 1dc in each st to end. (24)

Rnds 42-44: 1dc in each st to end. (24)

Add eyes, sew on a mouth.

Rnd 45: [dc2tog, 2dc] 6 times. (18)

Rnd 46: [dc2tog, 1dc] 6 times. (12)

Rnd 47: dc2tog until hole closes.

ARMS

(Make 2)

With flesh yarn

Rnd 1: 8dc in magic ring. (8)

Rnds 2-4: 1dc in each st to end. (8)

With gold yarn

Rnd 5: 1dc in each st to end. (8)

With black yarn

Rnd 6: 1dc in each st to end. (8)

With red yarn

Rnds 7-14: 1dc in each st to end. (8)

JACKET

With white yarn

Ch18

Row 1: 1htr in 3rd ch from hook, 14htr, 2htr in final st. (18)

Turn, and work into the bottom of the sts.

With red yarn

Row 2: 1ch, 1dc in next st, 2dc, 2dc in next st, [3dc, 2dc in next st] 3 times, turn. (20)

Rows 3-8: 1ch, 1dc in each st to end, turn. (20)

Row 9: 1ch, [4dc, 2dc in next st] 4 times, turn. (24)

Rows 10-12: 1ch, 1dc in each st to end, turn. (24)

Row 13: 1ch, [5dc, 2dc in next st] 4 times, turn. (28)

Rows 14-18: 1ch, 1dc in each st to end, turn. (28)

JACKET BORDER

With black yarn

Begin on the side of row 2, work along the 3 sides of jacket. 1ch, 1dc in each st until you get to a corner, 3dc in corner st, continue this along all three sides.

With gold yarn

Start a new row on top of the black border. 1ch, 2dc, 1htr, (spike into the work), 2dc, 1htr, continue until corner, 3dc into corner, 2dc, 1htr, work this pattern all the way around the three sides of the jacket, with 3dc into each corner.

CONSTRUCTION

Wrap jacket around body, and sew gold sides together. Attach arms.

Follow instructions for hair cap in brown, see page 125, sew on head.

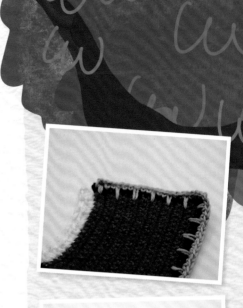

'I do love nothing in the world so well as you:
Is not that strange?'

Benedick (Act IV, Scene 1)

YARN

100% cotton 4ply in brown, flesh, white, yellow, orange, black

SUGGESTED YARN:

'Must-have' from Yarn and Colors: Taupe, Limestone, White, Golden Glow, Bronze, Black

OTHER MATERIALS

2.5 mm (C/2) crochet hook
Yarn needle
6 mm (1/3 in) safety eyes x 2
Stitch marker
Fibrefill stuffing

PATTERN NOTES

- For surface crochet instructions, see page 123.

- For htrcl stitch instructions, see page 124.

- For hair instructions, see page 125.

Beatrice

RIGHT LEG

With brown yarn

Rnd 1: 6ch, 1dc in 2nd ch from hook, 3dc, 4dc in next st, work remaining sts along the other side of the chs, 3dc, 3dc in next st, join. (14)

Work in spirals in continuous rounds without joining (unless otherwise stated), moving stitch marker up each round.

Rnd 2: 3dc, [2dc in next st] 4 times, 3dc, [2dc in next st] 4 times. (22)

Rnd 3 *in blo:* 3dc, [dc2tog] 4 times, 3dc, [dc2tog] 4 times. (14)

Rnd 4: 2dc, [dc2tog] 4 times, 1dc in each st to end. (10)

With flesh yarn

Rnd 5: 2dc, [dc2tog] twice, 1dc in each st to end. (8)

Rnds 6-13: 1dc in each st to end. (8)

LEFT LEG, BODY AND HEAD

With brown yarn

Rnd 1: 6ch, 1dc in 2nd ch from hook, 3dc, 4dc in next st, work remaining sts along the other side of the chs, 3dc, 3dc in next st, join. (14)

Work in spirals in continuous rounds without joining (unless otherwise stated), moving stitch marker up each round.

Rnd 2: 3dc, [2dc in next st] 4 times, 3dc, [2dc in next st] 4 times. (22)

Rnd 3 *in blo:* 3dc, [dc2tog] 4 times, 3dc, [dc2tog] 4 times. (14)

Rnd 4: 2dc, [dc2tog] 4 times, 1dc in each st to end. (10)

With flesh yarn

Rnd 5: 2dc, [dc2tog] twice, 1dc in each st to end. (8)

Rnds 6-13: 1dc in each st to end. (8)

With white yarn

Rnd 14: 4ch, join with a sl st to right leg, 1dc in each st around right leg, then continue 1dc in each st across chs, around left leg and across the other side of the chs. (24)

Rnds 15-19: 1dc in each st to end. (24)

Rnds 20-21 *in blo:* 1dc in each st to end. (24)

Rnds 22-27: 1dc in each st to end. (24)

Rnd 28: [4dc, dc2tog] 4 times. (20)

Rnd 29: 1dc in each st to end. (20)

Rnd 30: [3dc, dc2tog] 4 times. (16)

With orange yarn

Rnd 31: 1dc in each st to end. (16)

With flesh yarn

Rnd 32: [2dc, dc2tog] 4 times. (12)

Rnd 33: [1dc, dc2tog] 4 times. (8)

Rnd 34: 1dc in each st to end. (8)

Rnd 35: [2dc in next st, 1dc] 4 times. (12)

Rnd 36: 2dc in each st to end. (24)

Rnds 37-40: 1dc in each st to end. (24)

Rnd 41: 1dc in each st, until you get to the middle of the face, 4htrcl in next st, 1dc in each st to end. (24)

Rnds 42-44: 1dc in each st to end. (24)

Add eyes, sew on a mouth.

Rnd 45: [dc2tog, 2dc] 6 times. (18)

Rnd 46: [dc2tog, 1dc] 6 times. (12)

Rnd 47: dc2tog until hole closes.

TOP

With orange yarn

Ch16

Row 1: 1dc in 2nd ch from hook, 1dc in each st to end, turn. (15)

Row 2: 1ch, [2dc, 2dc in next st] 5 times, turn. (20)

Rows 3-10: 1ch, 1dc in next st to end, turn. (20)

Row 11: 1ch, [3dc, 2dc in next st] 5 times, turn. (25)

BORDER

With yellow yarn

Begin on the side of row 1, 1ch, 1dc in each st until you get to a corner, 3dc in the corner, continue this along the three sides of the top.

UNDERSKIRT

With yellow yarn

Turn Beatrice upside down and work into the front loops of round 20, join at any point.

Rnd 1: 2ch, 1htr in each st to end. (24)

Rnds 2-9: 2ch, 1htr in each st to end. (24)

OUTERSKIRT

With orange yarn

Keeping Beatrice turned upside down, work into the front loops of round 21, start from 2sts to the left of the middle.

Row 1: 2ch, 1htr in next st, 2htr in each st around, leave the last 2sts in the middle unworked, turn. (42)

Rows 2-8: 2ch, 1htr in each st to end, turn. (42)

Row 9: 2ch, 1htr, [with yellow yarn, 3htrcl, with orange yarn, 3htr] 9 times, with yellow yarn, 3htrcl, with orange yarn, 2htr, turn. (42)

Row 10: 2ch, 1htr in each st to end, turn. (42)

Row 11: 1ch, 1dc in each st to end. (42)

ARMS

(Make 2)

With flesh yarn

Rnd 1: 8dc in magic ring. (8)

Rnds 2-4: 1dc in each st to end. (8)

With white yarn

Rnds 5-14: 1dc in each st to end. (8)

SLEEVES

(Make 2)

With orange yarn

Ch3

Row 1: 7htr in first ch, turn. (8)

Row 2: 2ch, 2htr in each of the next 6 times, 1htr, turn. (14)

Row 3: 2ch, [2htr in next st, 1htr] 6 times, 2htr in next st, turn. (21)

Row 4: 2ch, 1htr in each st to end. (21)

Surface crochet with yellow across row 3.

CONSTRUCTION

Wrap top around body, and use black yarn to create a criss cross fastening. Add arms to body, and sew on sleeves.

See page 125 for hair instructions, in black.

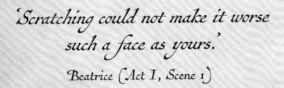

'Scratching could not make it worse such a face as yours.'

Beatrice (Act I, Scene 1)

The Tempest

*'We are such stuff as dreams are made on,
and our little life is rounded with a sleep.'*

Prospero (Act IV, Scene 1)

Prospero was once Duke of Milan, but was usurped by his brother
Antonio. Understandably annoyed, Prospero fled the city with his
daughter Miranda and settled on an enchanted island. He rules over
the spirit Ariel and the creature Caliban, the son of a witch. Years later,
Antonio, King Alonso of Naples and his son Ferdinand are sailing
nearby and Prospero conjures up a shipwreck to teach them a lesson.
Caliban meets Alonso's drunk butler, Stephano, and decides that he is his
new master. Mischief is made, Miranda and Ferdinand fall in love and
eventually Prospero and his brother reconcile. Prospero decides to go
back to Milan, leaving the island and magic forever.

Shakespeare's opening stage direction gives us an insight into the special
effects used by Jacobean playhouses in Shakespeare's time, 'a tempestuous
noise of thunder and lightning', which could have been created by
fireworks and thunder-sheets, or even a cannonball rolling down a trough.
The effect of a later direction, 'Enter Mariners, wet' would probably have
been created by a nearby stage-hand with a bucket of water!

YARN

PROSPERO

100% cotton 4ply in brown, flesh, light grey, grey, royal blue, optional: gold thread

SUGGESTED YARN:

'Must-have' from Yarn and Colors: Brownie, Limestone, Silver, Shark Grey, Sapphire

'Artiste Metallic' from Anchor: Gold

OTHER MATERIALS

2.5 mm (C/2) crochet hook
Yarn needle
6 mm safety eyes x 2
Stitch marker
Fibrefill stuffing

PATTERN NOTES

- For htrcl stitch instructions, see page 124.
- Make Prospero's hair according to the instructions on page 125, but use a variety of yarn lengths to give him the castaway look.

Prospero

TUNIC

With light grey yarn
Ch18, join with sl st to form a ring.
Rnd 1: 2ch, [2htr in next st, 1htr] 8 times, 2htr in next st, join. (27)
Rnds 2-13: 2ch, 1htr in each st to end, join. (27)

RIGHT LEG

With brown yarn
Rnd 1: 6ch, 1dc in 2nd ch from hook, 3dc, 4dc in next st, work remaining sts along the other side of the chs, 3dc, 3dc in next st, join. (14)

Work in spirals in continuous rounds without joining (unless otherwise stated), moving stitch marker up each round.
Rnd 2: 3dc, [2dc in next st] 4 times, 3dc, [2dc in next st] 4 times. (22)
Rnd 3 *in blo:* 3dc, [dc2tog] 4 times, 3dc, [dc2tog] 4 times. (14)
Fasten off brown yarn.
With flesh yarn
Rnd 4: 2dc, [dc2tog] 4 times, 1dc in each st to end. (10)
Rnd 5: 2dc, [dc2tog] twice, 1dc in each st to end. (8)
Rnds 6-13: 1dc in each st to end. (8)

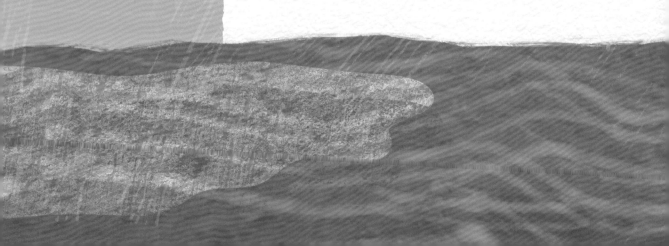

LEFT LEG, BODY AND HEAD

With brown yarn

Rnd 1: 6ch, 1dc in 2nd ch from hook, 3dc, 4dc in next st, work remaining sts along the other side of the chs, 3dc, 3dc in next st, join. (14)

Work in spirals in continuous rounds without joining (unless otherwise stated), moving stitch marker up each round.

Rnd 2: 3dc, [2dc in nex st] 4 times, 3dc, [2dc in next st] 4 times. (22)

Rnd 3 *in blo:* 3dc, [dc2tog] 4 times, 3dc, [dc2tog] 4 times. (14)

Fasten off brown yarn.

With flesh yarn

Rnd 4: 2dc, [dc2tog] 4 times, 1dc in each st to end. (10)

Rnd 5: 2dc, [dc2tog] twice, 1dc in each st to end. (8)

Rnds 6-13: 1dc in each st to end. (8)

Rnd 14: 4ch, and join with a sl st to right leg, 1dc in each st around right leg, then continue dcs across chs, around left leg, and across the other side of the chs. (24)

Rnds 15-19: 1dc in each st to end. (24)

Rnds 20 *in blo:* 1dc in each st to end. (24)

Rnds 21-27: 1dc in each st to end. (24)

Rnd 28: [4dc, dc2tog] 4 times. (20)

Rnd 29: 1dc in each st to end. (20)

Rnd 30: [3dc, dc2tog] 4 times. (16)

Rnd 31: 1dc in each st to end. (16)

Rnd 32: [2dc, dc2tog] 4 times. (12)

Rnd 33: [1dc, dc2tog] 4 times. (8)

Rnd 34: 1dc in each st to end. (8)

Rnd 35: [2dc in next st, 1dc] 4 times. (12)

Rnd 36: 2dc in each st to end. (24)

Rnds 37-40: 1dc in each st end. (24)

Rnd 41: 1dc in each st until you get to the middle of the face, 4htrcl in next st, 1dc in each st to end. (24)

Rnds 42-44: 1dc in each st to end. (24)

Add eyes and sew on mouth.

Rnd 45: [dc2tog, 2dc] 6 times. (18)

Rnd 46: [dc2tog, 1dc] 6 times. (12)

Rnd 47: dc2tog until hole closes.

BEARD

With light grey yarn

Ch16

Row 1: 1dc in 2nd ch from hook, 1dc in each st to end, turn. (15)

Row 2: 1ch, 5dc, 5ch, miss 5 sts, 1dc in each st to end, turn. (15)

Row 3: 1ch, 1dc in each st to end, turn. (15)

ARMS

(Make 2)

With flesh yarn

Rnd 1: 8dc in magic ring. (8)

Rnds 2-4: 1dc in each st to end. (8)

With light grey yarn

Rnds 5-14: 1dc in each st to end. (8)

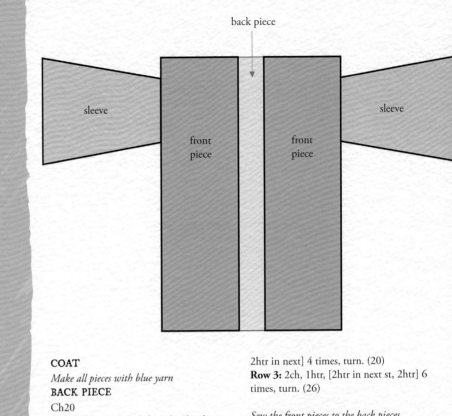

back piece

sleeve

front piece

front piece

sleeve

COAT
Make all pieces with blue yarn
BACK PIECE
Ch20
Row 1: 1htr in 3rd ch from hook, 1htr in each st to end, turn. (19)
Rows 2-14: 2ch, 1htr in each st to end, turn. (19)

FRONT PIECE
(Make 2)
Ch11
Row 1: 1htr in 3rd ch from hook, 1htr in each st to end, turn. (10)
Rows 2-14: 2ch, 1htr in each st to end, turn. (10)

SLEEVES
(Make 2)
Ch16
Row 1: 1htr in 3rd ch from hook, 1htr in each st to end, turn. (15)
Row 2: 2ch, 1htr, 2htr in next st, [2htr,

2htr in next] 4 times, turn. (20)
Row 3: 2ch, 1htr, [2htr in next st, 2htr] 6 times, turn. (26)

Sew the front pieces to the back pieces, leaving a gap on each st for the sleeves. Sew in the sleeves. Optional, sew a line with the gold thread on each of the front pieces.

CONSTRUCTION
See page 125 for hair instructions, make in light grey, with strands of varying lengths to give him a wilder look.
Sew on the beard.
Attach arms and add the coat.

STAFF
With brown yarn
Rnd 1: 6dc in magic ring. (6)
Rnd 2 *in blo:* 1dc in each st to end. (6)
Rnds 3-30: 1dc in each st to end. (6)
Rnd 31: dc2tog until hole closes.

YARN

CALIBAN

100% cotton 4ply in turquoise, green

SUGGESTED YARN:

'Must-have' from Yarn and Colors: Petroleum, Grass, Black, White

ARIEL

100% cotton 4ply in bright blue, light grey

SUGGESTED YARN:

'Must-have' from Yarn and Colors: Blue Lake, Silver

OTHER MATERIALS

2.5 mm (C/2) crochet hook
Yarn needle
6 mm safety eyes x 2
10 mm safety eyes x 2
Stitch marker
Fibrefill stuffing
PVA glue
Greaseproof paper

Caliban

FIN

(Make 2)

With turquoise yarn

Ch12

Row 1: 1tr in 4th ch from hook, [2tr in next st, 1tr] 4 times. (14)

Sew both pieces together to create the fin.

ARMS

(Make 2)

With green yarn

Rnd 1: 8dc in magic ring. (8)

Rnds 2-9: 1dc in each st to end. (8)

HEAD AND BODY

With green yarn

Rnd 1: 6dc in magic ring. (6)

Rnd 2: 2dc in each st to end. (12)

Rnd 3: [2dc in next st, 1dc] 6 times. (18)

Rnd 4: [2dc in next st, 2dc] 6 times. (24)

Rnds 5-10: 1dc in each st to end. (24)

Add eyes and eyebrows, sew on fin.

Rnds 11-13: 1dc in each st to end. (24)

Sew nostrils and mouth.

Rnd 14: [dc2tog, 2dc] 6 times. (18)

Rnd 15: [dc2tog, 1dc] 6 times. (12)

Rnd 16: [dc2tog, 1dc] 6 times. (8)

Fasten off green yarn, with turquoise yarn

Rnd 17: 2dc in each st to end. (16)

Rnd 18: [2dc in next st, 1dc] 8 times. (24)

Rnd 19: [3htrcl in next st, 1dc] 12 times. (24)

Rnd 20: 1dc in each st to end. (24)

Rnd 21: repeat rnd 19.

Rnd 22: repeat rnd 20.

Rnd 23: repeat rnd 19.

Rnd 24: repeat rnd 20.

Rnd 25: repeat rnd 19.

Rnd 26: repeat rnd 20.

Rnd 27: repeat rnd 19.

Rnd 28: repeat rnd 20.

Rnd 29: [dc2tog, 2dc] 6 times. (18)

Rnd 30: [dc2tog, 1dc] 6 times. (12)

Rnd 31: dc2tog until hole closes.

LEGS

(Make 2)

With green yarn

Rnd 1: 6ch, 1dc in 2nd ch from hook, 3dc, 4dc in next st, work remaining sts along the other side of the chs, 3dc, 3dc in next st, join. (14)

Work in spirals in continuous rounds without joining (unless otherwise stated), moving stitch marker up each round.

Rnd 2: 3dc, [2dc in next st] 4 times, 3dc, [2dc in next st] 4 times. (22)

Rnd 3 in blo: 3dc, [dc2tog] 4 times, 3dc, [dc2tog] 4 times. (14)

Rnd 4: 2dc, [dc2tog] 4 times, 1dc in each st to end. (10)

Rnd 5: 2dc, [dc2tog] twice, 1dc in each st to end. (8)

Rnds 6-10: 1dc in each st to end. (8)

CONSTRUCTION

Sew arms and legs onto the body.

PATTERN NOTES

- Whereas most of the patterns in this book start from the feet up, Caliban and Ariel start from the head and work down.
- Caliban uses slightly larger eyes than other characters in this book, but would work well with 6mm if that's all you have to hand.

Ariel

HEAD AND BODY

With blue yarn

Rnd 1: 6dc in magic ring. (6)
Rnd 2: 2dc in each st to end. (12)
Rnd 3: [2dc in next st, 1dc] 6 times. (18)
Rnds 4-6: 1dc in each to end. (18)
Rnd 7: 1dc in each st until you get to the middle of the face, 4htrcl in next st, 1dc in each st to end. (18)
Rnds 8-9: 1dc in each st to end. (18)
Add eyes.
Rnd 10: [dc2tog, 1dc] 6 times. (12)
Rnd 11: [dc2tog] 6 times. (6)
Rnd 12: 2dc in each st to end. (12)
Rnd 13: [2dc in next st, 1dc] 6 times. (18)
Rnds 14-22: 1dc in each st to end. (18)
Rnd 23: [dc2tog, 1dc] 6 times. (12)
Rnd 24: dc2tog until hole closes.

LEGS

(Make 2)

With blue yarn

Rnd 1: 6dc in magic ring. (6)
Rnds 2-12: 1dc in each st to end. (6)

ARMS

(Make 2)

With blue yarn

Rnd 1: 6dc in magic ring. (6)
Rnds 2-9: 1dc in each st to end. (6)

WINGS

(Make 2)

With light grey yarn

Start your slipknot 10 cm in.
Ch6, join with sl st
Rnd 1: 3ch, 15tr in ring. (16)
Rnd 2: 1ch, 1dc, 1ch, 1dc, 1ch, 1htr, 1ch, 1htr, 1ch, 1tr, 1ch, [1tr, 3ch, 1tr] in next st, 1ch, 1tr, 1ch, 1htr, 1ch, 1htr, 1ch, 1dc, 1ch, 1dc, sl st, leave the last 4sts unworked. (12)

CONSTRUCTION

Sew legs and arms onto body. With the wings on greaseproof paper, spread PVA glue on them and leave to harden overnight, then sew onto body.

> *'Merrily, merrily, shall I live now*
> *Under the blossom that hangs*
> *on the bough.'*
>
> Ariel (Act V, Scene 1)

Othello

*'Oh, beware, my lord, of jealousy!
It is the green-eyed monster which doth mock
The meat it feeds on.'*

Iago (Act III, Scene 3)

When the play begins, Othello, the Moor of Venice, has a great military record and has just secretly married Desdemona, who was enthralled by his stories of heroics. Iago is angry at having not been promoted by Othello so decides to stir up trouble. First, he informs Desdemona's father about the marriage in a crude and racist way, then begins to manipulate all around him to inflame Othello's jealousy. By the end of the play, Othello is so convinced by Iago's manoeuvres to make him believe that Desdemona has committed adultery that he murders her.

Around 1,000 black people lived in England by the end of the 16th century and in 1601 Queen Elizabeth made a proclamation on the expulsion of 'negroes and blackamoors' from the country – even though she had black people among her staff. The first actor to play Othello would have almost certainly been white actor Richard Burbage, wearing makeup and a wig made of black lamb's wool. It wasn't until Ira Aldridge in the 1830s that a black actor played the role. Although trailblazing at the time, it was still uncommon for black actors to play the role well into the 20th century – between 1930 and 1980, only four African-Caribbean actors played the role on stage in Britain.

YARN

100% cotton 4ply in black, mustard, turquoise, white, burgundy

SUGGESTED YARN:
'Must-have' from Yarn and Colors: Black, Gold, Petroleum, White, Burgundy

OTHER MATERIALS

2.5 mm (C/2) crochet hook
Yarn needle
6 mm (1/3 in) safety eyes x 2
Stitch marker
Fibrefill stuffing

PATTERN NOTES

- For htrcl stitch instructions, see page 124.
- For hair instructions, see page 125.

Othello

RIGHT LEG

With black yarn

Rnd 1: 6ch, 1dc in 2nd ch from hook, 3dc, 4dc in next st, work remaining sts along the other side of the chs, 3dc, 3dc in next st, join. (14)

Work in spirals in continuous rounds without joining (unless otherwise stated), moving stitch marker up each round.

Rnd 2: 3dc, [2dc in next st] 4 times, 3dc, [2dc in next st] 4 times. (22)

Rnd 3 *in blo*: 3dc, [dc2tog] 4 times, 3dc, [dc2tog] 4 times. (14)

Rnd 4: 2dc, [dc2tog] 4 times, 1dc in each st to end. (10)

Rnd 5: 2dc, [dc2tog] twice, 1dc in each st to end. (8)

Rnds 6-7: 1dc in each st to end. (8)

With gold yarn

Rnds 8-13: 1dc in each st to end. (8)

LEFT LEG, BODY AND HEAD

With black yarn

Rnd 1: 6ch, 1dc in 2nd ch from hook, 3dc, 4dc in next st, work remaining sts along the other side of the chs, 3dc, 3dc in next st, join. (14)

Work in spirals in continuous rounds without joining (unless otherwise stated), moving

stitch marker up each round.

Rnd 2: 3dc, [2dc in next st] 4 times, 3dc, [2dc in next st] 4 times. (22)

Rnd 3 *in blo*: 3dc, [dc2tog] 4 times, 3dc, dc2tog 4 times. (14)

Rnd 4: 2dc, [dc2tog] 4 times, 1dc in each st to end. (10)

Rnd 5: 2dc, [dc2tog] twice, 1dc in each st to end. (8)

Rnds 6-7: 1dc in each st to end. (8)

With gold yarn

Rnds 8-13: 1dc in each st to end. (8)

Rnd 14: 4ch, and join with a sl st to right leg, 1dc around right leg, then continue dcs across chs, around left leg, and across the other side of the chs. (24)

Rnds 15-18: 1dc in each st to end. (24)

With turquoise yarn

Rnds 19-27: 1dc in each st to end. (24)

Rnd 28: [4dc, dc2tog] 4 times. (20)

Rnd 29: 1dc in each st to end. (20)

Rnd 30: [3dc, dc2tog] 4 times. (16)

Rnd 31: 1dc in each st to end. (16)

Rnd 32: [2dc, dc2tog] 4 times. (12)

With flesh yarn

Rnd 33: [1dc, dc2tog] 4 times. (8)

Rnd 34: 1dc in each st to end. (8)

Rnd 35: [2dc in next st, 1dc] 4 times. (12)

Rnd 36: 2dc in each st to end. (24)

88

Rnds 37-40: 1dc in each st to end. (24)

Rnd 41: 1dc in each st, until you get to where the nose should be, 4htrcl in next st, 1dc in each st to end. (24)

Stitch on a beard with black yarn and and a mouth with burgundy.

With flesh yarn

Rnds 42-44: 1dc in each st to end. (24)

Attach eyes

Rnd 45: [dc2tog, 2dc] 6 times. (18)

Rnd 46: [dc2tog, 1dc] 6 times. (12)

Rnd 47: dc2tog to end, until hole closes.

TUNIC

With white yarn

Ch21

Row 1: 2tr in 4th ch from hook, 16htr, 3tr in last st. (22)

Fasten off, with burgundy yarn, turn the piece around and work into bottom of the sts.

Row 2: 2ch, 1htr, 2htr in next st, [2htr, 2htr in next st] 5 times, turn. (24)

Rows 3-6: 2ch, 1htr in each st to end, turn. (24)

Row 7: 2ch, 4htr, 2htr in next st, [5htr, 2htr in next st] 3 times, turn. (28)

Rows 8-11: 2ch, 1htr in each st to end, turn. (28)

TUNIC BORDER

With gold yarn

Row 1: begin at row 2 of the tunic, and work along the 3 sides of the piece, 1ch, 1dc in each st to corner st, 3dc in corner st, 1dc in each st to next corner, 3dc in corner st, 1dc in each st to the end of row.

ARMS

(Make 2)

With flesh yarn

Rnd 1: 8dc in magic ring. (8)

Rnds 2-4: 1dc in each st to end. (8)

With gold yarn

Rnd 5: 1dc in each st to end. (8)

With turquoise yarn

Rnds 6-14: 1dc in each st to end. (8)

SHOULDERS

(Make 2)

With maroon yarn

Ch4

Row 1: 1tr in 4th ch from hook, continue to work all remaining sts in this next st as follows: [*with mustard yarn*, 1tr, *with maroon yarn*, 2tr] 3 times, turn. (11)

Row 2: 3ch, 1tr, [*with gold yarn*, 1tr, with *maroon yarn*, 2tr] 3 times, turn. (11)

Row 3: *with gold yarn*, 1ch, 1dc in each st to end. (11)

Follow hair cap instructions on page 125, in black.

CONSTRUCTION

Sew hair cap on the head. Sew tunic onto body, attach arms and shoulders to body.

'She loved me for the dangers I had pass'd,
And I loved her that she did pity them
This only is the witchcraft I have used.'

Othello (Act I, Scene 3)

YARN

100% cotton 4ply in grey, light grey, flesh, brown, blue, red, white

SUGGESTED YARN:
'Must-have' from Yarn and Colors: Shark Grey, Peach, Brunet, Pacific Blue, Pepper, White

OTHER MATERIALS

2.5 mm (C/2) crochet hook
Yarn needle
6 mm (1/3 in) safety eyes x 2
Stitch marker
Fibrefill stuffing

PATTERN NOTES

- For surface crochet instructions, see page 123.
- For htrcl stitch instructions, see page 124.

Iago

RIGHT LEG

With grey yarn

Rnd 1: 6ch, 1dc in 2nd ch from hook, 3dc, 4dc in next st, work remaining sts along the other side of the chs, 3dc, 3dc in next st, join. (14)

Work in spirals in continuous rounds without joining (unless otherwise stated), moving stitch marker up each round.

Rnd 2: 3dc, [2dc in next st] 4 times, 3dc, [2dc in next st] 4 times. (22)

Rnd 3 *in blo*: 3dc, [dc2tog] 4 times, 3dc, [dc2tog] 4 times. (14)

Rnd 4: 2dc, [dc2tog] 4 times, 1dc in each st to end. (10)

Rnd 5: 2dc, [dc2tog] twice, 1dc in each st to end. (8)

Rnd 6-7: 1dc in each st to end.

With light grey yarn

Rnd 8 *in blo*: 1dc in each st to end. (8)

Rnds 9-13: 1dc in each to end. (8)

LEFT LEG, BODY AND HEAD

With grey yarn

Rnd 1: 6ch, 1dc in 2nd ch from hook, 3dc, 4dc in next st, work remaining sts along the other side of the chs, 3dc, 3dc in next st, join. (14)

Work in spirals in continuous rounds without joining (unless otherwise stated), moving stitch marker up each round.

Rnd 2: 3dc, [2dc in next st] 4 times, 3dc, [2dc in next st] 4 times. (22)

Rnd 3 *in blo*: 3dc, [dc2tog] 4 times, 3dc, [dc2tog] 4 times. (14)

Rnd 4: 2dc, [dc2tog] 4 times, 1dc in each st to end. (10)

Rnd 5: 2dc, [dc2tog] twice, 1dc in each st to end. (8)

Rnd 6-7: 1dc in each st to end.

With light grey yarn

Rnd 8 *in blo*: 1dc in each st to end. (8)

Rnds 9-13: 1dc in each st to end. (8)

Rnd 14: 4ch, and join with a sl st to right leg, 1dc around right leg, then continue dcs across chs, around left leg, and across the other side of the chs. (24)

Rnds 15-27: 1dc in each st to end. (24)

Rnd 28: [4dc, dc2tog] 4 times. (20)

Rnd 29: 1dc in each st to end. (20)

Rnd 30: [3dc, dc2tog] 4 times. (16)

Rnd 31: 1dc in each st to end. (16)

With flesh yarn

Rnd 32: [2dc, dc2tog] 4 times. (12)

Rnd 33: [1dc, dc2tog] 4 times. (8)

Rnd 34: 1dc in each st to end. (8)

Rnd 35: [2dc in next st, 1dc] 4 times. (12)

'But I will wear my heart upon my sleeve
For daws to peck at: I am not what I am.'

Iago (Act I, Scene 1)

Rnd 36: 2dc in each st to end. (24)
Rnds 37-40: 1dc in each st to end. (24)
Rnd 41: 1dc in each st, until you get to the middle, 4htrcl in next st, 1dc in each st to end. (24)
Rnds 42-44: 1dc in each st to end. (24)
Add eyes, sew on a mouth.
Rnd 45: [dc2tog, 2dc] 6 times. (18)
Rnd 46: [dc2tog, 1dc] 6 times. (12)
Rnd 47: dc2tog to end until hole closes.

BOOT CUFFS
With grey yarn
Hold Iago upside down, work stitches into front loops of rnd 8 on each of the legs.
Rnds 1-2: 1ch, 1dc in each st to end. (8)

TUNIC
With blue yarn
Ch17
Row 1: 1dc in 2nd ch from hook, 1dc in each st to end, turn. (16)
Row 2: 1ch, [3dc, 2dc in next st] 4 times, turn. (20)
Row 3: 1ch, 1dc in each st to end, turn. (20)
Row 4: 1ch, [3dc, 2dc in next st] 5 times, turn. (25)
Row 5: 1dc in each st to end, turn. (25)
Row 6: 1ch, [2dc in next st, 2dc] 8 times, 2dc in next st, turn. (34)
Rows 7-15: 1ch, 1dc in each st to end, turn. (34)
Use red to surface crochet lines along the tunic, see page 123 for instructions.

BORDER
Starting at the left side of row 1 and working down the side of the tunic, 1dc in each st, until corner, 2dc in corner, work across the bottom, then up on the other side of the tunic until you get to the right side of row 1.

COLLAR
With white yarn
Ch19
Row 1: 2tr in the 4th ch from hook, [2tr in next st] 14 times, 3tr in last st. (34)
Sew onto tunic.

ARMS
(Make 2)
With flesh yarn
Row 1: 8dc in magic ring. (8)
Rows 2-4: 1dc in each st to end. (8)
With red yarn
Row 5: 1dc in each st to end. (8)
With blue yarn
Rows 6-14: 1dc in each st to end. (8)

TROUSERS
With blue yarn
Ch30, join with a sl st
Rnds 1-7: 1ch, 1dc in each st to end. (30)
Left leg
Rnd 8: 1ch, 15dc, sl st in first st, leave the rest of the sts unworked for right leg. (15)
Rnds 9-11: 1ch, 14dc, sl st to join. (15)
Repeat from round 8 in the unworked stitches to make the right leg, sew up to create trousers.

CONSTRUCTION
For hair, follow hair cap instructions on page 125 using brown yarn, and sew on head. Sew the collar onto the tunic, and put on body. Add arms.

The Winter's Tale

'Exit, pursued by a bear.'

(Act III, Scene 3)

Perhaps the most famous of all Shakespeare's stage directions, in which Lord Antigonus, who has travelled from Sicilia to Bohemia with baby Perdita, meets his end at the claws of a bear. Antigonus is part of King Leontes' court, who wrongly accuses his wife of having an affair with his friend, King Polixenes of Bohemia. He assumes his daughter, Perdita, must be the result of the infidelity and tells Antigonus to abandon her in a desolate place.

Sadly, bear baiting was seen as entertainment by Elizabethan and Jacobean audiences, and the animals were kept in kennels along the Thames, chained and attacked by dogs, with onlookers placing bets on the result. It's not clear how Shakespeare's original productions used to stage this moment, although other productions at the time would have used bearskins as costumes.

YARN

100% cotton 4ply; light grey, light brown, maroon, black, gold, flesh, brown, khaki
100% acrylic faux fur yarn: brown

SUGGESTED YARN:

'Must-have' from Yarn and Colors: Shadow, Ecru, Red Wine, Black, Mustard, Rosé, Taupe, Olive
James C Brett Faux Fur: H5

OTHER MATERIALS

2.5 mm (C/2) crochet hook
3 or 4 mm hook
Yarn needle
6 mm (1/3 in) safety eyes x 2
Stitch marker
Fibrefill stuffing

PATTERN NOTES

- Everything is worked using the 2.5 mm hook, except the border on Antigonus' cape, which uses the larger hook.
- For htrcl stitch instructions, see page 124.

Antigonus

TUNIC

With maroon yarn
Ch18, join with sl st
Rnd 1: 2ch, [2htr in next st, 1htr] 8 times, 2htr in next st, join. (27)
Rnds 2-10: 2ch, 1htr in each st to end, join. (27)

BELT

With black yarn
Ch34
Row 1: 1dc in 2nd ch from hook, 1dc in each st to end, turn. (33)
Row 2: 1ch, 1dc in each st to end, turn. (33)

BUCKLE

With gold yarn
Ch10
Join with a sl st, sew onto belt.

BEARD

With brown yarn
Ch16
Row 1: 1dc in 2nd ch from hook, 1dc in each st to end, turn. (15)
Row 2: 1ch, 5dc, 5ch, miss 5 ch, 1dc in st, 4dc, turn. (15)
Rows 3-4: 1ch, 1dc in each st to end, turn. (15)

RIGHT LEG

With grey yarn
Rnd 1: 6ch, 1dc in 2nd ch from hook, 3dc, 4dc in next st, work remaining sts along the other side of the chs, 3dc, 3dc in next st, join. (14)
Work in spirals in continuous rounds without joining (unless otherwise stated), moving stitch marker up each round.
Rnd 2: 3dc, [2dc in next st] 4 times, 3dc, [2dc in next st] 4 times. (22)
Rnd 3 in blo: 3dc, [dc2tog] 4 times, 3dc, [dc2tog] 4 times. (14)
Rnd 4: 2dc, [dc2tog] 4 times, 1dc in each st to end. (10)
Rnd 5: 2dc, [dc2tog] twice, 1dc in each to end. (8)
Rnds 6-7: 1dc in each st to end. (8)
Fasten off grey yarn, with brown yarn
Rnd 8 in blo: 1dc in each st to end. (8)
Rnds 9-13: 1dc in each st to end. (8)

LEFT LEG, BODY AND HEAD

With grey yarn

Rnd 1: 6ch, 1dc in 2nd ch from hook, 3dc, 4dc in next st, work remaining sts along the other side of the chs, 3dc, 3dc in next st, join. (14)

Work in spirals in continuous rounds without joining (unless otherwise stated), moving stitch marker up each round.

Rnd 2: 3dc, [2dc in next st] 4 times, 3dc, [2dc in next st] 4 times. (22)

Rnd 3 *in blo*: 3dc, [dc2tog] 4 times, 3dc, [dc2tog] 4 times. (14)

Rnd 4: 2dc, [dc2tog] 4 times, 1dc in each st to end. (10)

Rnd 5: 2dc, [dc2tog] twice, 1dc in each st to end. (8)

Rnds 6-7: 1dc in each st to end. (8)

Fasten off grey yarn.

With light brown yarn

Rnd 8 *in blo*: 1dc in each st to end. (8)

Rnds 9-13: 1dc in each st to end. (8)

With brown yarn

Rnd 14: 4ch, and join with a sl st to right leg, 1dc around right leg, then continue dcs across chs, around left leg, and across the other side of the chs. (24)

Rnds 15-27: 1dc in each st to end. (24)

Rnd 28: [4dc, dc2tog] 4 times. (20)

Rnd 29: 1dc in each st to end. (20)

Rnd 30: [3dc, dc2tog] 4 times. (16)

Rnd 31: 1dc in each st to end. (16)

Rnd 32: [2dc, dc2tog] 4 times. (12)

Fasten off brown yarn.

With flesh yarn

Rnd 33: [1dc, dc2tog] 4 times. (8)

Rnd 34: 1dc in each st to end. (8)

Rnd 35: [2dc in next st, 1dc] 4 times. (12)

Add the buckle to the belt, put the tunic on the body, and add the belt.

Rnd 36: 2dc in each st to end. (24)

Rnds 37-40: 1dc in each st to end. (24)

Rnd 41: 1dc in each st, until you get to the middle of the face, 4htrcl in next st, 1dc in each st to end. (24)

Rnds 42-44: 1dc in each st to end. (24)

Add eyes and sew on beard.

Rnd 45: [dc2tog, 2dc] 6 times. (18)

Rnd 46: [dc2tog, 1dc] 6 times. (12)

Rnd 47: dc2tog until hole closes.

BOOT CUFFS

With grey yarn

Turn Antigonus upside down and work stitches into the front loops of rnd 8 of both legs.

Rnd 1: 2ch, 1htr in each st to end. (8)

ARMS

(Make 2)

With flesh yarn

Rnd 1: 8dc in magic ring. (8)

Rnds 2-4: 1dc in each st to end. (8)

With maroon yarn

Rnds 5-14: 1dc in each st to end. (8)

Sew onto sides of body.

Make hair cap in brown, see page 125, sew on head.

CAPE

With khaki yarn

Ch22

Row 1: 1htr in 3rd ch from hook, 1htr in each st to end, turn. (22)

Rows 2-15: 2ch, 1htr in each st to end, turn. (22)

Fasten off khaki, with faux fur yarn, crochet a border using larger hook.

1dc in each st all the way around, except at a corner, 3dc in corner st.

> *'A savage clamour!*
> *Well may I get aboard! This is the chase:*
> *I am gone for ever.'*
>
> Antigonus (Act III, Scene 3)

The Bear

EARS

(Make 2)
With brown yarn
Rnd 1: 6dc in magic ring, turn. (6)
Rnd 2: 1ch, 1dc in each st to end. (6)

SNOUT

With brown yarn
Rnd 1: 6dc in magic ring. (6)
Rnd 2: [2dc in next st, 1dc] 3 times. (9)
Rnds 3-4: 1dc in each st to end. (9)
Rnd 5: [2dc in next st, 2dc] 3 times. (12)
Rnd 6: 1dc in each st to end. (12)
Use the black yarn to sew on a little nose.

HEAD

With brown yarn
Rnd 1: 8dc in magic ring. (8)
Rnd 2: 2dc in each st to end. (16)
Rnd 3: [2dc in next st, 1dc] 8 times. (24)
Rnd 4: [2dc in next st, 2dc] 8 times. (32)
Rnds 5-11: 1dc in each st to end. (32)
Sew on ears and snout, add eyes.
Rnds 12-13: 1dc in each st to end. (32)
Rnd 14: [2dc, dc2tog] 8 times. (24)
Rnd 15: [1dc, dc2tog] 8 times. (16)

BODY

With brown yarn
Rnd 1: 6dc in magic ring. (6)
Rnd 2: 2dc in each st to end. (12)
Rnd 3: [2dc in next st, 1dc] 6 times. (18)
Rnd 4: [2dc in next st, 2dc] 6 times. (24)
Rnd 5: [2dc in next st, 3dc] 6 times. (30)
Rnds 6-28: 1dc in each st to end. (30)
Rnd 29: [dc2tog, 3dc] 6 times. (24)
Rnd 30: 1dc in each st to end. (24)
Rnd 31: [dc2tog, 2dc] 6 times. (18)
Rnd 32: 1dc in each st to end. (18)
Rnd 33: [dc2tog, 1dc] 6 times. (12)
Rnd 34: dc2tog until hole closes.
Sew head onto body.

ARMS

(Make 2)
With brown yarn
Rnd 1: 6dc in magic ring. (6)
Rnd 2: [1dc, 2dc in next st] 3 times. (9)
Rnds 3-4: 1dc in each st to end. (9)
Rnd 5: [dc2tog, 1dc] 3 times. (6)
Rnds 6-13: 1dc in each st to end. (6)
Use grey yarn to sew lines to make paws, stuff and sew on to body.

LEGS

(Make 2)
With brown yarn
Rnd 1: 8dc in magic ring. (8)
Rnd 2: 2dc in each st to end. (16)
Rnd 3 *in blo*: 1dc in each st to end. (16)
Rnd 4: 1dc in each st to end. (16)
Use grey yarn to sew lines to make paws, stuff and sew onto body.
Rnd 5: 5dc, [dc2tog] 3 times, 5dc. (13)
Rnds 6-12: 1dc in each st to end. (13)
Use the grey yarn to sew lines to make paws, stuff and sew on to body.

YARN

100% cotton 4ply; brown, scrap amount of black, optional scrap amounts of grey

SUGGESTED YARN:
'Must-have' from Yarn and Colors: Brownie, Black, Shark Grey

OTHER MATERIALS

2.5 mm (C/2) crochet hook
Yarn needle
6 mm (1/3 in) safety eyes x 2
Stitch marker
Fibrefill stuffing

PATTERN NOTES

- Using wire is not recommended on the bear as each of the pieces is individual.

'Grrrrrrrr.....'

The Bear (Act III, Scene 3)

The Merry Wives of Windsor

'O powerful Love, that in some respects makes a beast a man, in some other a man a beast.'

Falstaff (Act V, Scene 5)

Sir John Falstaff is down on his luck financially and thinks he'll be able to change his fortunes by pursuing the wives of two rich merchants, Mistress Page and Mistress Ford. The ladies find out he's trying to romance them both at the same time, and so they plot to make mischief at Falstaff's expense. During the course of the play, Falstaff is thrown into a river, forced to dress as an old woman and also gets beaten up. In the final act, they lure him to Windsor Park with the promise of a romantic liaison. At their request, Falstaff dresses as Herne the Hunter, an English folklore character said to have antlers growing from his head. The ladies stage an evening of supernatural goings-on before their scheme is revealed.

The comical character, Falstaff, appears in both *Henry IV*, Part 1 and Part 2, and is memorialised in *Henry V*. The character is thought to have been such a favourite of Queen Elizabeth I that she requested to see him in love and Shakespeare wrote *The Merry Wives of Windsor* in order to satisfy the monarch's wishes. The play was a hit, and has been adapted as an opera numerous times including by composers Verdi and Salieri.

YARN

100% cotton 4ply in black, khaki, brown, grey, flesh, mustard, and scrap yarn in any colour

SUGGESTED YARN:
'Must-have' from Yarn and Colors: Black, Olive, Brownie, Shark Grey, Peach, Gold

OTHER MATERIALS

2.5 mm (C/2) crochet hook
Yarn needle
6 mm (1/3 in) safety eyes x 2
Stitch marker
Fibrefill stuffing

PATTERN NOTES

- As Falstaff is low on cash in this play, his clothes are deliberately mismatched, you may decide to change the colours so he's a bit more co-ordinated.

- For htrcl stitch instructions, see page 124.

Falstaff

RIGHT LEG
With black yarn
Rnd 1: 6ch, 1dc in 2nd ch from hook, 3dc, 4dc in next st, work remaining sts along the other side of the chs, 3dc, 3dc in next st, join. (14)
Work in spirals in continuous rounds without joining (unless otherwise stated), moving stitch marker up each round.
Rnd 2: 3dc, [2dc in next st] 4 times, 3dc, [2dc in next st] 4 times. (22)
Rnd 3 *in blo*: 3dc, [dc2tog] 4 times, 3dc, [dc2tog] 4 times. (14)
Rnd 4: 2dc, [dc2tog] 4 times, 1dc in each st to end. (10)
With white yarn
Rnd 5: 2dc, [dc2tog] twice, 1dc in each st to end. (8)
Rnds 6-7: 1dc in each st to end. (8)
With khaki yarn
Rnd 8 *in blo*: 1dc in each st to end. (8)
Rnds 9-13: 1dc in each st to end. (8)

LEFT LEG, BODY AND HEAD
With black yarn
Rnd 1: 6ch, 1dc in 2nd ch from hook, 3dc, 4dc in next st, work remaining sts along the other side of the chs, 3dc, 3dc in next st, join. (14)

Work in spirals in continuous rounds without joining (unless otherwise stated), moving stitch marker up each round.
Rnd 2: 3dc, [2dc in next st] 4 times, 3dc, [2dc in next st] 4 times. (22)
Rnd 3 *in blo*: 3dc, [dc2tog] 4 times, 3dc, [dc2tog] 4 times. (14)
Rnd 4: 2dc, [dc2tog] 4 times, 1dc in each st to end. (10)
With white yarn
Rnd 5: 2dc, [dc2tog] twice, 1dc in each st to end. (8)
Rnd 6-7: 1dc in each st to end. (8)
With khaki yarn
Rnd 8 *in blo*: 1dc in each st to end. (8)
Rnds 9-13: 1dc in each st to end. (8)
Rnd 14: 4ch, and join with a sl st to right leg, 1dc around right leg, then continue dcs across chs, around left leg, and across the other side of the chs. (24)
Rnd 15: 1dc in each st to end. (24)
Rnd 16: [2dc in next st] twice, 16dc, [2dc in next st] 3 times, 2dc, 2dc in next st. (30)
Rnd 17: 1dc, [2dc in next st, 1dc] twice, 15dc, [2dc in next st, 1dc] three times, 3dc, 2dc in next st. (36)
Rnds 18-26: 1dc in each st to end. (36)
Rnd 27: [dc2tog, 4dc] 6 times. (32)

Rnd 28: 1dc in each st to end. (32)
Rnd 29: [dc2tog, 2dc] 8 times. (24)
Rnds 30-33: 1dc in each st to end. (24)
Rnd 34: [1dc, dc2tog] 8 times. (16)
Rnds 35-36: 1dc in each st to end. (16)
With flesh yarn
Rnd 37: [dc2tog] 8 times. (8)
Rnd 38: [2dc in next st, 1dc] 4 times. (12)
Rnd 39: 2dc in each st to end. (24)
Rnds 40-43: 1dc in each st to end. (24)
Rnd 44: 1dc in each st, until you get to the middle of the face, 4htrcl in next st, 1dc in each st to end. (24)
Rnds 45-47: 1dc in each st to end. (24)
Sew on beard and use the red yarn to sew a mouth.
Attach eyes.
Rnd 48: [dc2tog, 2dc] 6 times. (18)
Rnd 49: [dc2tog, 1dc] 6 times. (12)
Rnd 50: dc2tog until hole closes.

BEARD
With grey yarn
Ch16
Row 1: 1dc in 2nd ch from hook, 1dc in each st to end, turn. (15)
Row 2: 5dc, 5ch, miss 5 sts, 1dc in each st to end, turn. (15)
Rows 3-4: 1ch, 1dc in each st to end, turn. (15)

HAIR
With grey yarn
Leave a long tail at the start to sew
Ch16
Row 1: 1htr in 3rd ch from hook, 1htr in each st to end, turn. (15)
Row 2: 2ch, [2htr in next st, 1htr] 7 times, turn. (22)
Rows 3-6: 1htr in each st to end, turn. (22)
Sew row 1 along the back of Falstaff's head.

TROUSERS
With brown yarn
Ch40, join with a sl st to form a ring.
Rnds 1-10: 1ch, 1dc in each st to end, join. (40)

Put around waist and sew a few stitches in the middle to join the front and back and make into trousers.

JACKET
With white yarn
Ch24
Row 1: 2tr in 4th ch from hook, 18tr, 3tr in last st, turn. (24)
Row 2: 3ch, 2tr in first st, 22tr, 3tr in last st. (30)
Fasten off, turn and work into the bottom of the sts of row 1.
With gold yarn
Row 3: 1ch, 1dc in each st to end, turn. (20)
Row 4: 1ch, [3dc, 2dc in next st] 5 times, turn. (25)
Row 5: 1ch, [4dc, 2dc in next st] 5 times, turn. (30)
Rows 6-9: 1ch, 1dc in each st to end, turn. (30)
Row 10: 1ch, [4dc, 2dc in next st] 6 times, turn. (36)
Row 11: 1ch, [5dc, 2dc in next st] 7 times, turn. (42)
Rows 12-18: 1ch, 1dc in each st to end, turn. (42)

ARMS
(Make 2)
With flesh yarn
Rnd 1: 8dc in magic ring. (8)
Rnds 2-4: 1dc in each st to end. (8)
With white yarn
Rnds 5-14: 1dc in each st to end. (8)

PATCHES
(Make 3-4 with scraps)
Ch4
Row 1: 1dc in 2nd ch from hook, 2dc, turn. (3)
Rows 2-3: 1ch, 3dc, turn. (3)

CONSTRUCTION
Sew patches onto trousers and shirt, using black yarn. Wrap shirt around body, and sew up from row 8-18. Sew arms to the side of body. Sew beard onto face.

'I think the devil will not have me damned, lest the oil that's in me should set hell on fire.'

Falstaff (Act V, Scene 5)

YARN

100% cotton 4ply in black, flesh, white, dark green, burgundy

SUGGESTED YARN:
'Must-have' from Yarn and Colors: Black, Taupe, Forest, Burgundy

OTHER MATERIALS

2.5 mm (C/2) crochet hook
Yarn needle
6 mm (1/3 in) safety eyes x 2
Stitch marker
Fibrefill stuffing

PATTERN NOTES

• For htrcl stitch instructions, see page 124.

Mistress Page

RIGHT LEG

With black yarn

Rnd 1: 6ch, 1dc in 2nd ch from hook, 3dc, 4dc in next st, work remaining sts along the other side of the chs, 3dc, 3dc in next st, join. (14)

Work in spirals in continuous rounds without joining (unless otherwise stated), moving stitch marker up each round.

Rnd 2: 3dc, [2dc in next st] 4 times, 3dc, [2dc in next st] 4 times. (22)

Rnd 3 *in blo:* 3dc, [dc2tog] 4 times, 3dc, [dc2tog] 4 times. (14)

Rnd 4: 2dc, [dc2tog] 4 times, 1dc in each st to end. (10)

Rnd 5: 2dc, [dc2tog] twice, 1dc in each st to end. (8)

With flesh yarn

Rnds 6-13: 1dc in each st to end. (8)

LEFT LEG, BODY AND HEAD

With black yarn

Rnd 1: 6ch, 1dc in 2nd ch from hook, 3dc, 4dc in next st, work remaining sts along the other side of the chs, 3dc, 3dc in next st, join. (14)

Work in spirals in continuous rounds without joining (unless otherwise stated), moving stitch marker up each round.

Rnd 2: 3dc, [2dc in next st] 4 times, 3dc, [2dc in next st] 4 times. (22)

Rnd 3 *in blo:* 3dc, [dc2tog] 4 times, 3dc, [dc2tog] 4 times. (14)

Rnd 4: 2dc, [dc2tog] 4 times, 1dc in each st to end. (10)

Rnd 5: 2dc, [dc2tog] twice, 1dc in each st to end. (8)

With flesh yarn

Rnds 6-13: 1dc in each st to end. (8)

With white yarn

Rnd 14: 4ch, join with a sl st to right leg, 1dc in each st around right leg, then continue 1dc in each st across chs, around left leg and across the other side of the chs. (24)

Rnds 15-19: 1dc in each st to end. (24)

Rnds 20 *in blo:* 1dc in each st to end. (24)

Rnds 21-27: 1dc in each st to end. (24)

Rnd 28: [4dc, dc2tog] 4 times. (20)

Rnd 29: 1dc in each st to end. (20)

Rnd 30: [3dc, dc2tog] 4 times. (16)

Rnd 31: 1dc in each st to end. (16)

With flesh yarn

Rnd 32: [2dc, dc2tog] 4 times. (12)

Rnd 33: [1dc, dc2tog] 4 times. (8)

Rnd 34: 1dc in each st to end. (8)

Rnd 35: [2dc in next st, 1dc] 4 times. (12)

Rnd 36: 2dc in each st to end. (24)

Rnds 37-40: 1dc in each st to end. (24)

Rnd 41: 1dc in each st, until you get to the middle of the face, 4htrcl in next st, 1dc in each st to end. (24)

Rnds 42-44: 1dc in each st to end. (24)

Add eyes, sew on a mouth.

Rnd 45: [dc2tog, 2dc] 6 times. (18)

Rnd 46: [dc2tog, 1dc] 6 times. (12)

Rnd 47: dc2tog to end until hole closes.

UNDERSKIRT

With white yarn

Work into the front loops of round 20, begin at the back for neatness.

Rnd 1: 2ch, [2htr in next st, 1htr] 11 times, 2htr in next st. (36)

Rnds 2-9: 2ch, 1htr in each st to end. (36)

Rnd 10: [2ch, slst in next st, 1sl st in next st] 18 times.

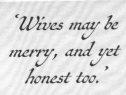

'Wives may be
merry, and yet
honest too.'

Mistress Page
(Act IV, Scene 2)

ARMS

(Make 2)

With flesh yarn

Rnd 1: 8dc in magic ring. (8)

Rnds 2-4: 1dc in each st to end. (8)

With white yarn

Rnds 5-14: 1dc in each st to end. (8)

DRESS

With white yarn

Ch16

Row 1: 2tr in 4th ch from hook, 11htr, 3tr in last ch (17)

Turn the piece upside down and work the next row into the bottom of the sts.

With green yarn

Rows 2-3: 1ch, 1dc in each st to end, turn. (13)

Row 4: 1ch, [1dc, 2dc in next st] 6 times, 1dc, turn. (19)

Rows 5-6: 1ch, 1dc in each st to end, turn. (19)

Row 7: 1ch, [1dc in st, 2dc in next st] 8 times, 1dc, turn. (28)

Rows 8-15: 1ch, 1dc in each st to end, turn. (28)

Row 16: 1ch, [1dc, 2dc in next st] 13 times, 1dc, turn. (41)

Rows 17-30: 1ch, 1dc in each st to end, turn. (41)

BORDER

With burgundy yarn

Start at the right side of row 2 and work down the side of the dress, dcs all the way down, 3dcs in corner st, and continue along the bottom, 3dcs in corner st, work up the other side of the dress.

Make a small st to pinch the dress in at the waist.

ARMS

(Make 2)

With flesh yarn

Rnd 1: 8dc in magic ring. (8)

Rnd 2-4: 1dc in each st to end. (8)

With green yarn

Rnd 5 *in blo*: 1dc in each st to end. (8)

Rnds 6-14: 1dc in each st to end. (8)

CUFFS

(Make 2)

With white yarn

Work into the front loops of rnd 5, 2ch, [2htr in next st] 7 times, 1htr in the same st as starting chs. (16)

BUN

With black yarn

Rnd 1: 6dc in magic ring. (6)

Rnd 2: 2dc in each st to end. (12)

Rnd 3: [2dc in next st, 1dc] 6 times. (18)

Rnds 4-5: 1dc in each st to end. (18)

Make the hair cap as the instructions on page 125, with black.

Add stuffing and sew onto hair cap.

Sew hair onto head.

YARN

100% cotton 4ply in black, flesh, light grey, blue, red, orange, white

SUGGESTED YARN:
'Must-have' from Yarn and Colors: Black, Peach, Silver, Sapphire, Pepper, Bronze, White

OTHER MATERIALS

2.5 mm (C/2) crochet hook
Yarn needle
6 mm (1/3 in) safety eyes x 2
Stitch marker
Fibrefill stuffing

PATTERN NOTES

- For Mistress Ford's dress, join with a sl st at the end of each round.
- For htrcl stitch instructions, see page 124.
- For surface crochet instructions, see page 123.
- flo means work into front loops only.

Mistress Ford

DRESS

With blue yarn
Ch16, join with a sl st to make a ring.
Rnd 1: 1ch, [1dc, 2dc in next st] 8 times, join. (24)
Rnds 2-3: 1ch, 1dc in each st to end, join. (24)
Rnd 4: 1ch, [3dc, 2dc in next st] 6 times, join. (30)
Rnds 5-13: 1ch, 1dc in each st to end, join. (30)
Rnd 14: 1ch, [1dc, 2dc in next st] 15 times, join. (45)
Rnd 15: 1ch, [2dc, 2dc in next st] 15 times, join. (60)
Rnds 16-28: 1ch, 1dc in each st to end, join. (60)
Rnd 29: [with blue yarn, 1ch, 3dc, with red yarn, 3htrcl] 15 times, join. (60)
Rnd 30: with blue yarn, 1ch, 1dc in each st to end, join. (60)
Rnd 31: with red yarn, 1ch 1dc in each st to end, join. (60)
Rnd 32: with blue yarn, 1ch, 1dc in each st to end, join. (60)

CUFFS

(Make 2)
With white yarn
Ch4
Row 1: 1dc in 2nd ch from hook, 2dc, turn. (3)
Rows 2-13 in blo: 1ch, 1dc in each st to end, turn. (3)
Sew onto arms at wrist.

RUFF

With white yarn
Ch6
Row 1: 1dc in 2nd ch from hook, 3dc, 1htr, turn. (5)
Row 2 in blo: 1ch, 1dc in each st to end, turn. (5)
Row 3 in blo: 1ch, 4dc, 1htr, turn. (5)
For all even number rows, rep row 2, for all odd number rows rep row 3, continue in this way until row 30.
Fasten off leaving a few cms of yarn, sew row 30 to row 1 to make a round collar.

RIGHT LEG

With black yarn
Rnd 1: 6ch, 1dc in 2nd ch from hook, 3dc, 4dc in next st, work remaining sts along the other side of the chs, 3dc, 3dc in next st, join. (14)
Work in spirals in continuous rounds without joining (unless otherwise stated), moving stitch marker up each round.

Rnd 2: 3dc, [2dc in next st] 4 times, 3dc, [2dc in next st] 4 times. (22)
Rnd 3 in blo: 3dc, [dc2tog] 4 times, 3dc, [dc2tog] 4 times. (14)
Rnd 4: 2dc, [dc2tog] 4 times, 1dc in each st to end. (10)
Rnd 5: 2dc, [dc2tog] twice, 1dc in each st to end. (8)
With flesh yarn
Rnds 6-13: 1dc in each st to end. (8)

LEFT LEG, BODY AND HEAD
With black yarn
Rnd 1: 6ch, 1dc in 2nd ch from hook, 3dc, 4dc in next st, work remaining sts along the other side of the chs, 3dc, 3dc in next st, join. (14)
Work in spirals in continuous rounds without joining (unless otherwise stated), moving stitch marker up each round.
Rnd 2: 3dc, [2dc in next st] 4 times, 3dc, [2dc in next st] 4 times. (22)
Rnd 3 in blo: 3dc, [dc2tog] 4 times, 3dc, [dc2tog] 4 times. (14)
Rnd 4: 2dc, [dc2tog] 4 times, 1dc in each st to end. (10)
Rnd 5: 2dc, [dc2tog] twice, 1dc in each st to end. (8)
With flesh yarn
Rnds 6-13: 1dc in each st to end. (8)
With light grey yarn
Rnd 14: 4ch, join with a sl st to right leg, 1dc in each st around right leg, then continue 1dc in each st across chs, around left leg and across the other side of the chs. (24)
Rnds 15-27: 1dc in each st to end. (24)
Rnd 28: [4dc, dc2tog] 4 times. (20)
Rnd 29: 1dc in each st to end. (20)
Rnd 30: [3dc, dc2tog] 4 times. (16)
With flesh yarn
Rnd 31: 1dc in each st to end. (16)

Rnd 32: [2dc, dc2tog] 4 times. (12)
Rnd 33: [1dc, dc2tog] 4 times. (8)
Rnd 34: 1dc in each st to end. (8)
Rnd 35: [2dc in next st, 1dc] 4 times. (12)
Rnd 36: 2dc in each st to end. (24)
Add dress and ruff.
Rnds 37-40: 1dc in each st to end. (24)
Rnd 41: 1dc in each st, until you get to the middle of the face, 4htrcl in next st, 1dc in each st to end. (24)
Rnds 42-44: 1dc in each st to end. (24)
Add eyes, sew on a mouth.
Rnd 45: [dc2tog, 2dc] 6 times. (18)
Rnd 46: [dc2tog, 1dc] 6 times. (12)
Rnd 47: dc2tog to end until hole closes.

HEADDRESS
With blue yarn
Ch30
Row 1: 1htr in 3rd ch from hook, 7htr, [2tr in next st] 4 times, [3tr in next st] twice, [2tr in next st] 4 times, 1htr in each st to end, turn. (30)
Row 2 in flo: 2ch *(doesn't count as st)*, 8htr, tr2tog 11 times, 8htr. (38)
With red yarn, surface crochet across the front.

ARMS
(Make 2)
With flesh yarn
Rnd 1: 8dc in magic ring. (8)
Rnds 2-4: 1dc in each st to end. (8)
With blue yarn
Rnds 5-9: 1dc in each st to end. (8)
With red yarn
Rnds 10-14: 1dc in each st to end. (8)
Sew arms onto body.

Make hair in orange, following instructions on page 125. Sew onto head.

'How shall I be revenged on him? I think the best way were to entertain him with hope till the wicked fire of lust have melted him in his own grease!'
Mistress Ford (Act I, Scene 2)

Twelfth Night

'If music be the food of love, play on.'

Duke Orsino (Act I, Scene 1)

Washed up in a shipwreck, Viola assumes her twin brother Sebastian has drowned. She decides she must find employment to support herself so she disguises herself as a man and calls herself Cesario. Cesario manages to find work as Duke Orsino's messenger, who is trying to woo Olivia. However, Viola falls in love with Orsino, and Olivia falls in love with Cesario. It turns out Sebastian hasn't drowned and when he bumps into Olivia, she assumes he's Cesario and proposes to him. Eventually, the disguise is revealed, the siblings are reunited and Orsino falls for Viola.

Female characters in Shakespeare's time would have been played by boys, and the particular trope of a boy playing a woman who is pretending to be a man was known as 'the female page'. We see this in many of his other plays including *As You Like It*, *Two Gentlemen of Verona* and *The Merchant of Venice*. Since then, many acting greats have played the part of Viola on stage and screen including Judi Dench and Diana Rigg, (before they were Dames), and Zöe Wanamaker, Helen Hunt and Anne Hathaway. Harking back to the Elizabethan traditions, a fresh-faced Eddie Redmayne made his professional stage debut as Viola for the Globe Theatre in 2002.

YARN

100% cotton 4ply in white, black, light blue, turquoise, brown, flesh

SUGGESTED YARN:

'Must-have' from Yarn and Colors: White, Black, Opaline, Blue Lake, Brownie, Limestone

OTHER MATERIALS

2.5 mm (C/2) crochet hook
Yarn needle
6 mm (1/3 in) safety eyes x 2
Stitch marker
Fibrefill stuffing

PATTERN NOTES

- This pattern has been designed so that the character can change quickly from Viola to Cesario, by swapping the skirt for trousers, and the headdress for a hat.
- For hair instructions, see page 125.
- For htrcl stitch instructions, see page 124.

Viola / Cesario

RIGHT LEG

With brown yarn

Rnd 1: 6ch, 1dc in 2nd ch from hook, 3dc, 4dc in next st, work remaining sts along the other side of the chs, 3dc, 3dc in next st, join. (14)

Work in spirals in continuous rounds without joining (unless otherwise stated), moving stitch marker up each round.

Rnd 2: 3dc, [2dc in next st] 4 times, 3dc, [2dc in next st] 4 times. (22)

Rnd 3 *in blo:* 3dc, [dc2tog] 4 times, 3dc, [dc2tog] 4 times. (14)

Rnd 4: 2dc, [dc2tog] 4 times, 1dc in each st to end. (10)

Fasten off brown yarn.

With white yarn

Rnd 5: 2dc, [dc2tog] twice, 1dc in each st to end. (8)

Rnds 6-13: 1dc in each st to end. (8)

Fasten off

LEFT LEG, BODY AND HEAD

With brown yarn

Rnd 1: 6ch, 1dc in 2nd ch from hook, 3dc, 4dc in next st, work remaining sts along the other side of the chs, 3dc, 3dc in next st, join. (14)

Work in spirals in continuous rounds without joining (unless otherwise stated), moving stitch marker up each round.

Rnd 2: 3dc, [2dc in next st] 4 times, 3dc, [2dc in next st] 4 times. (22)

Rnd 3 *in blo:* 3dc, [dc2tog] 4 times, 3dc, [dc2tog] 4 times. (14)

Rnd 4: 2dc, [dc2tog] 4 times, 1dc in each st to end. (10)

Fasten off brown yarn.

With white yarn

Rnd 5: 2dc, [dc2tog] twice, 1dc in each st to end. (8)

Rnds 6-13: 1dc in each st to end. (8)

Rnd 14: 4ch, and join with a sl st to right leg, 1dc around right leg, then continue dcs across chs, around left leg, and across the other side of the chs. (24)

Rnds 15-27: 1dc in each st to end. (24)

Rnd 28: [4dc, dc2tog] 4 times. (20)

Rnd 29: 1dc in each st to end. (20)

Rnd 30: [3dc, dc2tog] 4 times. (16)

Rnd 31: 1dc in each st to end. (16)

Rnd 32: [2dc, dc2tog] 4 times. (12)

Rnd 33: [1dc, dc2tog] 4 times. (8)

Fasten off white yarn.

With flesh yarn

Rnd 34: 1dc in each st to end. (8)

Rnd 35: [2dc in st, 1dc] 4 times. (12)
Rnd 36: 2dc in each st to end. (24)
Rnds 37-40: 1dc in each st to end. (24)
Rnd 41: 1dc in each st until you get to the middle of the head, 4htrcl in next st, 1dc to end. (24)
Rnds 42-44: 1dc in each st to end. (24)
Add eyes and a mouth.
Rnd 45: [dc2tog, 2dc] 6 times. (18)
Rnd 46: [dc2tog, 1dc] 6 times. (12)
Rnd 47: dc2tog until hole closes.

VIOLA'S SKIRT

With light blue yarn
Ch30, join with sl st
Rnd 1: 1ch, 1dc in each st, join. (30)
Fasten off light blue yarn.
With turquoise yarn
Rnd 2: 2ch, [2htr in next st, 1htr] 14 times, 2htr in next st, join. (45)
Rnds 3-12: 2ch, 1htr in each st to end, join. (45)
Rnd 13: 2ch, 1htr, [*with light blue yarn*, 3htrcl in next st, *with turquoise yarn*, 2htr] 14 times, *with light blue yarn*, 3htrcl in next st, join. (45)
Rnd 14: 1ch, 1dc in each st, join. (45)

CESARIO'S TROUSERS

With light blue yarn
Ch30, join.
Rnd 1: 1ch, 1dc in each st to end, join. (30)
Fasten off light blue yarn.
With turquoise yarn
Rnds 2-6: 2ch, 1htr in each st to end, join. (30)
For right leg:
Rnd 7: 2ch, 14htr, join with sl st to the top of the starting chs, leave the rest of the sts unworked, they be will for the left leg. (25)
Rnd 8: 2ch, 1htr in each st to end, join. (15)
Fasten off turquoise yarn.
With light blue yarn
Rnd 9: 1ch, 1dc in each st to end, join. (15)
Fasten off.

For left leg:
Rnd 7: *rejoin turquoise to this round,* 2ch, 14htr around the remaining unworked sts, join. (15)
Rnd 8: 2ch, 1htr in each st, join. (15)
Fasten off turquoise yarn.
With light blue yarn
Rnd 9: 1ch, 1dc in each st to end, join. (15)

JACKET

With white yarn
Ch17
Row 1: 1htr in 3rd ch from hook, turn. (16)
Fasten off white yarn.
With turquoise yarn
Row 2: 2ch, 2htr, 2htr in next st, [3htr, 2htr in next st] 3 times, turn. (20)
Row 3: 2ch, 1htr in each st to end, turn. (20)
Row 4: 2ch, 2htr, 2htr in next st, [3htr, 2htr in next st] 4 times, turn. (25)
Row 5: 2ch, 3htr, 2htr in next st, [4htr, 2htr in next st] 4 times, turn. (30)
Rows 6-7: 2ch, 1htr in each st to end, turn. (30)

BORDER

With light blue yarn
Row 1: begin at row 2, and work along the 3 sides of the jacket of the 1ch, 1dc in each st to corner st, 3dc in corner st, 1dc in st to next corner, 3dc in corner st, 1dc in each st to end.
Place jacket on figure and sew on.

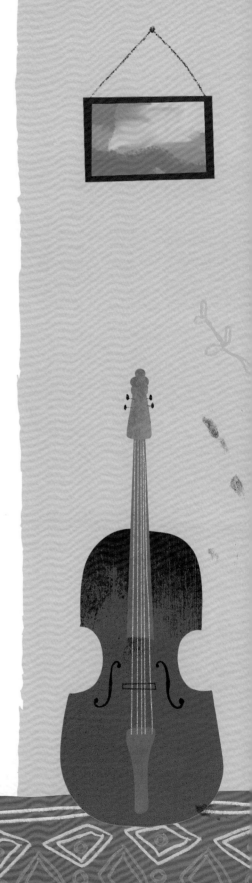

Row 2: 1ch, 1dc in each st to end. (11)
Sew onto top of shoulders.

*Make hair with brown yarn, see page 125
for instructions, and sew on head.*

VIOLA'S HEADDRESS
Piece 1
With light blue yarn
Ch32, join with a sl st.
Rnd 1: 1ch, [1dc, 2dc in next st]
16 times, join. (48)
Rnds 2-3: 1ch, 1dc in each st to end,
join. (48)
*Fasten off, leave a long tail for sewing,
fold and sew rnd 3 and rnd 1 together,
to make a thick loop.*
Piece 2
With turquoise yarn
Ch90
*Leave a long tail. Wrap around the piece 1
evenly and sew in.*

CESARIO'S HAT
With black yarn
Ch4
Rnd 1: 7htr in 4th ch from hook, join
with a sl st. (8)
Rnd 2: 2ch, 2htr in each st, 1htr in the
same st as starting ch, join. (16)
Rnd 3: 2ch, 2htr in each st, 1htr in the
same st as starting ch, join. (32)
Rnd 4 *in blo:* 1ch, 1dc in each st to end,
do not join. (32)
Rnds 5-12: 1dc in each st to end, do not
join. (32)
Rnd 13: 2ch, 1htr, [2htr in next st, 2htr]
10 times, join. (42)
Rnd 14: 2ch, 1htr, [2htr in next st, 2htr]
13 times, 2htr in next st, join. (56)

ARMS
With flesh yarn
Rnd 1: 8dc in magic ring. (8)
Rnds 2-4: 1dc in each st to end. (8)
Fasten off flesh yarn, with white yarn
Rnds 5-14: 1dc in each st to end. (8)
Sew to sides of body.

SHOULDERS
(Make 2)
With turquoise yarn
Row 1: Ch4, 1tr in first ch, work all
subsequent stitches in the first ch,
[*with light blue yarn,* 1tr, *with turquoise
yarn* 1tr] 4 times, *with turquoise yarn,*
1tr, don't join. (11)
*Fasten off turquoise yarn, leaving enough
yarn for sewing onto body.*
*Rejoin light blue yarn on the next side,
and at the start of row 1.*

> 'O time, thou must untangle this, not I.
> It is too hard a knot for me t'untie.'
>
> Viola (Act II, Scene 2)

Woolliam Shakespeare

'Shall I compare thee to a Summer's Day?'

Sonnet 18

Shakespeare wrote at least 37 plays, 150 sonnets, lived through plague and was successful in his own lifetime as a writer and actor, and his appeal has not faded in the centuries since his death. Born in 1564 in Stratford-upon-Avon, England, William was the eldest son of John Shakespeare, a prosperous glover, and Mary Arden, daughter of a wealthy farmer. He married at 18 and had three children with his wife, Anne.

While his family stayed in Stratford, Shakespeare moved to London and became an actor and writer for his own troupe – the Lord Chamberlain's Men, named after their aristocratic sponsor. They performed for audiences at the Globe Theatre, along the River Thames as well as for Queen Elizabeth I. After the Queen died and King James took over the throne, Shakespeare's players became 'The King's Men'.

Nowadays, you can still visit houses where Shakespeare lived in Stratford-upon-Avon and visit a recreation of the Globe Theatre along the Thames.

YARN

100% cotton 4ply in black, grey, white, gold, flesh

SUGGESTED YARN:

'Must-have' from Yarn and Colors: Black, Shark Grey, White, Mustard, Rosé

OTHER MATERIALS

2.5 mm (C/2) crochet hook
Yarn needle
6 mm (1/3 in) safety eyes x 2
Stitch marker
Fibrefill stuffing

PATTERN NOTES

• For htrcl stitch instructions, see page 124.

The Bard

RIGHT LEG

With black yarn

Rnd 1: 6ch, 1dc in 2nd ch from hook, 3dc, 4dc in next st, work remaining sts along the other side of the chs, 3dc, 3dc in next st, join. (14)

Work in spirals in continuous rounds without joining (unless otherwise stated), moving stitch marker up each round.

Rnd 2: 3dc, [2dc in next st] 4 times, 3dc, [2dc in next st] 4 times. (22)

Rnd 3 *in blo*: 3dc, [dc2tog] 4 times, 3dc, [dc2tog] 4 times. (14)

Rnd 4: 2dc, [dc2tog] 4 times, dc to end. (10)

Rnd 5: 2dc, [dc2tog] twice, dc to end. (8)

Rnds 6-7: 1dc in each st to end. (8)

With grey yarn

Rnd 8 *in blo*: 1dc in each st to end. (8)

Rnds 9-13: 1dc in each st to end. (8)

LEFT LEG, BODY AND HEAD

With black yarn

Rnd 1: 6ch, 1dc in 2nd ch from hook, 3dc, 4dc in next st, work remaining sts along the other side of the chs, 3dc, 3dc in next st, join. (14)

Work in spirals in continuous rounds without joining (unless otherwise stated), moving stitch marker up each round.

Rnd 2: 3dc, [2dc in next st] 4 times, 3dc, [2dc in next st] 4 times. (22)

Rnd 3 *in blo*: 3dc, [dc2tog] 4 times, 3dc, [dc2tog] 4 times. (14)

Rnd 4: 2dc, [dc2tog] 4 times, dc to end. (10)

Rnd 5: 2dc, [dc2tog] twice, dc to end. (8)

Rnds 6-7: 1dc in each st to end. (8)

With grey yarn

Rnd 8 *in blo*: 1dc in each st to end.(8)

Rnds 9-13: 1dc in each st to end. (8)

Fasten off.

Rnd 14: 4ch, and join with a sl st to right leg, 1dc around right leg, then continue dcs across chs, around left leg, and across the other side of the chs. (24)

Rnds 15-19: 1dc in each st to end. (24)
Rnd 20 *in blo*: 1dc in each st to end. (24)
Rnds 21-27: 1dc in each st to end. (24)
Rnd 28: [4dc, dc2tog] 4 times. (20)
Rnd 29: 1dc in each st to end. (20)
Rnd 30: [3dc, dc2tog] 4 times. (16)
Rnd 31: 1dc in each st to end. (16)
With flesh yarn –
Rnd 32: [2dc, dc2tog] 4 times. (12)
Rnd 33: [1dc, dc2tog] 4 times. (8)
Rnd 34: 1dc in each st to end. (8)
Rnd 35: [2dc in next st, 1dc] 4 times. (12)
Rnd 36: 2dc in each st to end. (24)
Rnds 37-40: 1dc in each st to end. (24)
Rnd 41: 1dc in each st until you get to the middle of the face, 4htrcl in next st, 1dc in each st to end. (24)
Use the black yarn to sew on a moustache and beard, use red yarn to sew on a mouth.
Rnds 42-44: 1dc in each st to end. (24)
Attach eyes.
Rnd 45: [dc2tog, 2dc] 6 times. (18)
Rnd 46: [dc2tog, 1dc] 6 times. (12)
Rnd 47: dc2tog to end, until hole closes.

HAIR
With black yarn
Ch16
Row 1: 1htr in 3rd ch from hook, 1htr in each st to end, turn. (15)
Row 2: 2ch, [2htr in next st, 1htr] 7 times, turn. (22)
Rows 3-4: 2ch, 1htr in each st to end, turn. (22)
Sew to the head.

BOOT CUFFS
With black yarn
Turn Woolliam upside down, work into the front loops of rnd 8 on the leg.
Rnd 1: 2ch, 1htr in each st to end, join with a sl st to starting chs. (8)
Repeat for the other leg.

COLLAR
With white yarn
Ch16
Row 1: 1tr in 3rd ch from hook, 2tr in each st to end, turn. (28)
Row 2: 2ch, 2htr in next st [1htr, 2htr in next st] 13 times. (42)

JACKET
With black yarn
Ch16
Row 1: 1tr in 4th ch from hook, 1tr to end, turn. (13)

Rows 2-10: 3ch, 1tr in each st to end, turn. (13)
Fasten off black.
With gold yarn
Row 11: you'll be working 3 sides of the rectangle you've made, 1ch, 1dc in each st until you get to a corner, 3dc in corner st, 1dc in each st along the longer side of the rectangle, 3dc in corner st, 1dc in each st to end.
Wrap around body and sew at border.

TROUSERS
With black yarn
Start in the front loops of rnd 20 on the body, begin at the middle of the back.
Rnd 1: 1ch, 1dc in each st to end, join with sl st. (24)
Rnd 2: 2ch, 1htr in each st to end, join with sl st. (24)
Rnd 3: 2ch, 4htr, 2htr in next st, [5htr, 2htr in next st] 3 times, join with sl st. (28)
Rnds 4-5: 2ch, 1htr in each st to end, (28)
Rnd 6: 2ch, 12htr, fasten off, miss st and then refasten the yarn, 2ch, 12htr, fasten off. (26)
Add a few stitches to form trousers.

ARMS
(Make 2)
With flesh yarn
Rnd 1: 8dc in magic ring. (8)
Rnds 2-4: 1dc in each st to end. (8)
With black yarn
Rnds 5-14: 1dc in each st to end. (8)

CUFFS
(Make 2)
With white yarn
Ch10, join with sl st
Row 1: 2ch, 1htr in next st, 2htr in each st to end, join with sl st. (20)
Sew to the end of arm, sew arms to the side of the body.

SHOULDERS
(Make 2)
With black yarn
Row 1: 4ch, 1tr in first ch, work subsequent stitches in the first ch, [*with gold*, 1tr, *with black*, 1tr] 4 times, *with black,* 1tr, turn. (11)
Row 2: *with gold,* 1ch, 1dc in each st to end. (11)
Add to the top of the arms.

How to Crochet

If you've never crocheted before, or you're brushing up on skills that have lain dormant for years, please be patient with yourself – crochet wasn't built in a day! Get comfortable with some of the basic techniques first before you start a project. I've provided a guide here, but you may also find video tutorials helpful too. You'll find some on my website: yayforcrochet.com. If you're completely new to crochet, I'd recommend playing around and getting comfortable with stitches and the techniques before starting with a pattern.

Holding Your Hook

There are two ways to hold a hook, the pencil position and the knife position. If you're new to crochet it's worth trying both positions out and seeing which is more comfortable. The hook is held in your dominant hand.

Pencil position

Hold the hook as you would if it was a pencil around 3-5 cms from the tip, or if your hook has a thumb rest, hold it here.

Knife position

Hold the hook as if you were cutting up food with a table knife, around 3-5 cms from the tip, or if your hook has a thumb rest, hold it here.

Pencil position

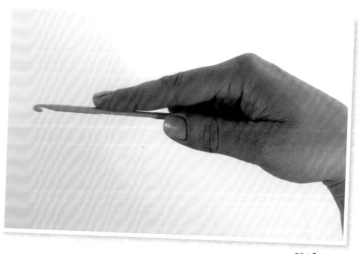

Knife position

Magic Ring

Also known as an adjustable loop, and used for a lot of patterns in the book.

1

At around 10 cm from the yarn end, wrap the yarn twice around your index and middle fingers.

2

Insert hook under both loops, pull the yarn closest to your knuckles under the other one.

3

Use your dominant hand to take the yarn off your fingers, while keeping the shape.

4

Hold the loose ring with the thumb and middle finger of your non-dominant hand, wrap the yarn around the hook and pull through (as if you are creating a chain).

5

Follow the instructions in your pattern and crochet all the stitches into the loose ring. Join with a sl st if required in the pattern.

6

When you've finished the pattern instructions, pull the yarn end and the ring will tighten. I would recommend doing a little knot so that the ring doesn't unravel.

Tip: If you're really struggling with this (and many people do!) just do 2 chs at the start of your work and crochet the stitches into the first chain. You may need to tighten this up with a needle.

Slip Knot

Unless it says start with a magic ring, start with a slip knot. Make a loop with the yarn.

Take the piece that is on top and fold it underneath the loop.

Pull this piece through the loop to create the slip knot.

Put the crochet hook into the loop and pull the yarn end so that the loop is close to the hook but not too tight. Check that you can still move the hook easily.

Holding Your Yarn

The yarn is held with your non-dominant hand.

My preferred method for holding yarn is as to hold your hand as if you are about to click your fingers. There are other methods so see which is the most comfortable for you.

At around 20 cm from the yarn end, hold this to your palm with your little finger and ring finger, securely but not so tight that you can't pull up the yarn.

Hang the yarn on your index finger and bring your thumb and middle finger in to pinch the yarn just under the slip knot.

As your work progresses, your index finger and thumb should move along to just under the loop your crochet hook is in.

Chain Stitch
(abbreviation: ch)

After you've started with a slip knot, hold the hook in your dominant hand, wrap the yarn around the hook so it is gripped by the tip.

Pull this yarn through your slip knot.

Continue to create chs with this method, wrapping the yarn around the hook and pulling this through the loop that is already on your hook. They will look like a small plait.

Slip Stitch
(abbreviation: sl st)

Slip stitches are used to join rounds or to move to another point on your work.

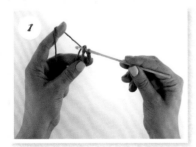

Insert the hook into the stitch.

Wrap the yarn around the tip of the hook.

Pull the yarn through the stitch and the loop on the hook.

Double Crochet
(single crochet in US) (abbreviation: dc)

This stitch will be the one that you mostly use throughout the book.

Insert the hook into the stitch.

Wrap the yarn around the hook.

Pull this through the stitch. You will now have two loops on the hook.

Wrap the yarn over the hook again and pull this through both loops.

Half Treble Crochet
(half double crochet in US) (abbreviation: htr)

Wrap the yarn around the hook.

Insert the hook into the stitch.

Wrap the yarn around the hook and pull it through the stitch. You will now have three loops on the hook.

Wrap the yarn around the hook and pull it through all three loops.

In your pattern, two chains at the start of a row count as a half treble.

Treble Crochet
(double crochet in US) (abbreviation: tr)

Wrap the yarn around the hook.

Insert the hook into the stitch.

Wrap the yarn around the hook and pull it through the stitch. You will now have three loops on the hook.

Wrap the yarn around the hook and pull it through the first two loops.

You will now have two loops on your hook. Wrap the yarn around the hook and pull this through both loops.

In your pattern, three chains at the start of a row count as a treble.

Double Treble Crochet
(treble crochet in the US) (abbreviation: dtr)

Wrap the yarn around the hook twice.

Insert the hook into the stitch. Wrap the yarn around the hook, and pull through. You will now have four loops on your hook.

Wrap the yarn around the hook and pull through the first two loops.

You will now have three loops on your hook, wrap the yarn around the hook, and pull through the first two loops.

You will now have two loops on your hook, wrap the yarn around the hook and pull it through both loops.

In your pattern, four chains at the start of a row count as a double treble.

Decreasing and Increasing

If the pattern reads 2dc in the next st, or something similar, this is an increase. Work these double crochets into the same stitch in the previous row. The number of stitches at the end of a row or round should also increase, so it's worth having a quick count at the end.

If the pattern reads dc2tog, or something similar, this is a decrease. Start a double crochet in one stitch, but instead of finishing the stitch insert your hook into the next stitch, pull the yarn through so you should have three loops on your hook and then finish the stitch. The number of stitches at the end of the row or round should also decrease, so it's worth having a quick count at the end.

Back Loops Only
(abbreviation: blo)

When you are crocheting you normally put your hook through the two loops of a stitch. When you need to do back loops only, find the one loop at the back of the stitch and put your hook through this one only. Occasionally, you'll work into front loops too.

Working in the Round

Many of the patterns in this book are worked using the traditional amigurumi technique of working in a continuous spiral without joining.

The pattern will state if you need to join with a sl st at the end. If it doesn't it means you'll be working in spirals. When you get to the end of a round, continue the first stitch of the next round on top.

Working in Rows

Some of the clothes in the book are worked using rows, which means that unless otherwise stated, you'll need to turn at the end of a row and work your stitches across.

Embroidery Chain Stitch

This stitch is borrowed from embroidery and is good for adding a little embellishment to clothes.

Thread a tapestry needle with the desired yarn and secure the end with a knot. Now, pull the needle through your crocheted 'fabric' from the back to the front. should close, leaving a small shape. Continue these steps to create chains.

Create a loop, and work your needle into the fabric, very close to where the yarn emerged in step 1. Bring the needle up through the fabric a few millimetres forward, making sure that the loop is sitting underneath the tip of the needle as you pull the yarn through.

Now make another loop and place your needle inside the previous loop and repeat this process from step 2 to create your row of chains.

Surface Crochet

Surface crochet will produce a similar effect to the embroidery chain stitch and is easy to master.

Insert the hook (without the yarn attached) into the front of your 'fabric' where the surface stitches will start.

At the back of your fabric, attach the slip knotted yarn onto your hook. The slipknot should remain at the back but bring the loop through the front. The tail of your yarn should also be at the back of your work.

Insert the hook into the fabric a little further on (the size of a double crochet).

At the back, wrap the yarn around the hook, and pull this through.

There will be two loops on your hook, so pull the loop you've just received through the original loop.

You've created something that looks like a chain on top of your work, repeat the process as per the pattern.

Loop Stitch (*abbreviation ls*)

Insert the hook into the stitch, and create a loop with the yarn that is wrapped around your finger, keeping both ends close together.

Pull the side of the loop through the stitch.

You'll have two loops on your hook. Take your finger out from the large loop at the back and hold your work as you would normally.

Wrap the yarn around the hook, and pull it through the two small loops. The large loop at the back should be secure and not change size with gentle pulling.

Half Treble Cluster Stitches (*abbreviation: htrcl*)

This stitch will be written with a number at the front, eg 4htrcl which is mostly used for noses, but you'll also see 3htrcl and 2htrcl appear in the book.

Begin as you would a htr, ie. wrap the yarn around the hook, insert into the stitch, wrap the yarn around the hook, pull through and you'll now have 3 loops on your hook.

Instead of finishing the htr, repeat the process as if you are making another htr, ie. wrap the yarn around the hook, insert into the stitch, wrap the yarn around the hook, and pull through. You will now have five loops on your hook. For a 2htrcl, wrap the yarn around the hook and pull through all seven loops.

For 3htrcl, repeat the htr process again, and you'll have seven loops on your hook. Wrap the yarn around the hook and pull through all seven loops.

For 4htrcl, repeat the htr process again, so you'll have nine loops on your hook. Wrap the yarn around the hook and pull through all nine loops.

Hair

There are many ways to attach hair to a figure, this is my preferred method which is fairly quick and easy. I've used different colours for the hair and the hair cap to demonstrate the effect.

Short hair

Make a hair cap

Rnd 1: 6dc in magic ring. (6)

Rnd 2: 2dc in each st to end. (12)

Rnd 3: [2dc in next st, 1dc] 6 times. (18)

Rnd 4: [2dc in next st, 2dc] 6 times. (24)

Rnds 5-8: 1dc in each st to end. (24)

For Romeo, Antony, Caesar, Brutus and Iago there is an additional round:

Rnd 9: sl st, 3ch, 1dc in first ch from hook, miss 1 in rnd 8, sl st in next, sl st to neaten. (24)

Long hair

The length and look of the hair will very much depend on your character, eg Prospero will look better with hair of varying lengths as he's been living on a desert island for years, whereas many of the ladies will require a neater look.

First make a hair cap in the desired colour as shown in the instructions for short hair. Rounds 1-8. Leave a long tail for sewing onto the head.

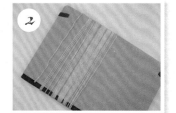

Wrap the yarn 30 times around a book – for long hair I would recommend the width of an A5 notebook.

Cut at one side, so you have 30 strands of hair. Take two strands at a time and knot them together in the middle.

With the knot on the inside of the hair cap, pull the strands through to top of the hair cap.

Repeat at various points around the haircap. You may want to add more strands (repeat steps 2 and 3) to give the hair a fuller look.

Sew onto the head at a 45-degree angle. Trim the hair to neaten it.

How to Read a Pattern

To the untrained eye, crochet patterns can look quite daunting.
Once you know how to decode them they are fairly easy to read.

Unless the pattern says to use a magic ring,
always start with a slip knot.

6ch – start your pattern
with 6 chain stitches.

3dc – work 1 double
crochet in each of the next
3 stitches or chs.

3dc – a number and a
stitch means that you
crochet 1 double crochet in
each of the next 3 stitches.

in blo – all the stitches
in this row/round should
be worked into the back
loops of the stitches in the
previous row/round, 'in
flo', means all stitches in
this row/round should be
worked into the front loops
of the previous row/round.

1dc in 2nd ch from hook –
work 1 double crochet into
the second chain along.

4dc in next st – work
4 double crochets into
the next st.

join – join with a slip stitch
to the top of the starting
chains.

[2dc in next st] 4 times –
square brackets indicate
that this section should be
repeated however many
times stated.

(22) – the number in the
brackets indicates how
many stitches there are in
the row or round you have
just worked.

Example:

Rnd 1: 6ch, 1dc in 2nd ch from hook,
3dc, 4dc in next st, work remaining
sts along the other side of the chs,
3dc, 3dc in next st, join. (14)

*For the remaining rounds do not join
unless otherwise stated. Place a stitch
marker in the first stitch of a round.*

Rnd 2: 3dc, [2dc in next st] 4 times,
3dc, [2dc in next st] 4 times. (22)

Rnd 3 in blo: 3dc, [dc2tog] 4 times,
3dc, dc2tog 4 times. (14)

Rnd 4: 3ch, 1tr in each st to end. (14)

3ch – the first chs at the start of a row
or round give you the height you'll
need, 3 chains count as 1 treble, 2
chains count as a half treble. 1ch at
the start of a round doesn't count as a
st, so work a dc in to the same st.

1tr in each st to end – carry
on this stitch until the end
of the row or round.

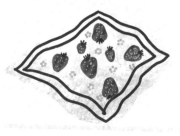

Tension

Tension is not hugely necessary in these patterns as the finished sizing isn't particularly important, and everyone will make their stitches at slightly different sizes. The tension for all the patterns is 13 stitches and 13 rows measured over 5 x 5 cm square over dc using a 2.5 mm crochet hook. If you want to check, crochet a square swatch that is slightly larger than 5 x 5 cm (2 x 2 in). Measure 5 cm and see if you have the same number of stitches that is stated at the start of the pattern. If you have more stitches than specified in the pattern your tension is too tight and you'll need to increase the size of your hook. If you have fewer stitches than stated, you'll need to use a slightly smaller hook. Create another tension swatch to test again.

Sizing

Using the suggested yarn and hooks, the average height for the characters is 15 cm.

Charts

Charts provide a visual representation of the patterns and are a useful guide when crocheting. Example: This chart shows the pattern opposite.

Conversion Table
(abbreviations)

This book is written using UK terminology. If you're looking at tutorials on the internet, check which country's terms they are using so you don't end up with completely the wrong stitches in your work.

UK term	US term
Chain (ch)	Chain (ch)
Slip stitch (sl st)	Slip stitch (sl st)
Double crochet (dc)	Single crochet (sc)
Half treble crochet (htr)	Half double crochet (hdc)
Treble crochet (tr)	Double crochet (dc)
Double treble crochet (dtr)	Treble crochet (tr)

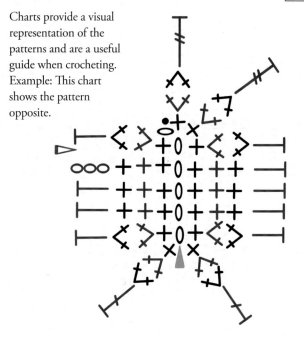

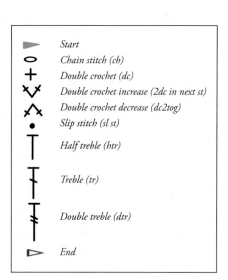

▶	Start
o	Chain stitch (ch)
+	Double crochet (dc)
⋎	Double crochet increase (2dc in next st)
⋏	Double crochet decrease (dc2tog)
•	Slip stitch (sl st)
T	Half treble (htr)
╫	Treble (tr)
╪	Double treble (dtr)
▷	End

Acknowledgements

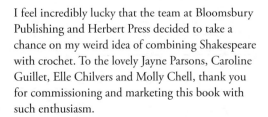

'I can no other answer make but thanks,
And thanks, and ever thanks.'

Sebastian, *Twelfth Night* (Act III, Scene 3)

I feel incredibly lucky that the team at Bloomsbury Publishing and Herbert Press decided to take a chance on my weird idea of combining Shakespeare with crochet. To the lovely Jayne Parsons, Caroline Guillet, Elle Chilvers and Molly Chell, thank you for commissioning and marketing this book with such enthusiasm.

The fantastic Plum 5 put this entire book together, and I'm so glad to be working again with Dave Macartney and Andy Chapman. Andy, you deserve a medal for your incredible patience with me throughout this process.

Heaps of appreciation go to Amelia Best, her fabulous illustrations which have given the characters their beautiful backdrops, what a talent! Thank you to Andy Smart, for your fantastic photography skills that brought my little *dramatis personae* to life… the kids thank you for your hot chocolate making skills too.

Thank you to Najiyah Abdin and Nikol Deehan for their additional photography talents and making my hands look nice! Big love and thanks to Tiana Lea for making it happen.

My rambling patterns would be nothing without Rachel Vowles and her tech editing wizardry, thank you for ensuring that things made sense.

To my wonderful friends, Dr Nooreen Khan, Jessye Emmerson, Steven Brown and Alan Dudman. Thank you for cheering me on, providing fun and ensuring that I still had a semblance of a social life when I could have easily spent every second of every day crocheting figures.

I'm not sure if they'll ever even see this, but I'd like to thank the English and Drama department of King Edward VI Camp Hill School for Girls between 1992-1999. You first introduced me to Shakespeare, and it was there I developed my love for the Bard and theatre, and it's had a lasting impact. I'm fortunate to have been taught by such a passionate group of women.

Masses of gratitude to my family for all their love, Dad, Rani, Bobby, Shane, Kierthan, Rajan, Jayan, Sampuran, Tara, Allan, Brenda, Faye, Laura, Matt and Lauren.

Special appreciation to my mum, Amarjit Birdi, for teaching me how to crochet and also just how to do about a million and one other things. Without you none of this would have happened.

To my children, Maya and Rishi, my two mini Shakespeare fans, who've been my little sidekicks while I went to Shakespeare plays, talks about Tudor costumes, visited Tudor houses and read lots of Shakespeare-related stuff. You've both been an absolute joy throughout, bursting with ideas and so incredibly sweet and understanding through this entire process, especially when I've been distracted and busy.

To my leading man, Kev, who has been my sounding board for ideas and just the most supportive husband I could ever have asked for. Thank you for all the patience when balls of yarn, needles and hooks take up most of the house, as well as all the pep talks and ridiculous amounts of laughs. As Miranda said to Ferdinand, 'I would not wish any companion in the world but you.'